Learn GIS Programming
with ArcGIS Javascript API 4.x and
ArcGIS Online

Hussein Nasser

For my wife, Nada

About the Author

My name is Hussein and I'm a software engineer. I specialize in the field of geographic information systems (or GIS). Since 2005, I helped many organizations in different countries implement GIS technology and wrote custom apps to fit their use cases and streamline their workflows. I wrote five books on Esri ArcGIS technology, recorded over two hundred GIS and programming YouTube videos and tutorials watched until this day and started a software engineer podcast in 2018. I've been an engineer at Esri building cool GIS products since 2015.

First published 2018
Last updated Feb 2019

Table of Contents

Preface

In late 2012 I got an email from a book publisher author with a proposal to author a book. They have found me through my blog and linked a blog post I wrote back in 2009 on ArcGIS Server technology. I accepted their offer and wrote the book and 3 others that followed.

This makes me question, why did I write that original blog post? I didn't know that one day a publisher will google that technology and find my post and make me an offer to write a book. I can't remember why exactly I wrote that post but I knew that I was having fun doing it. Sharing my experience with the world through this writing always felt good to me.

Most of you might have found this book through my YouTube channel, IGeometry, where I discuss software engineering topics and GIS in particular. In August 2017 I started a new series called Getting Started with ArcGIS Javascript API 4.x on YouTube. That series became really popular. The interaction on that series inspired me to write this book to discuss things I might have missed in that video series and to distill all my findings, knowledge into a book. So if you are new to the YouTube channel consider subscribing to check out more content over there https://www.youtube.com/igeometry

Today, I decided to re-live the experience of writing a book. However, no publisher is backing up this book. This book is written from the heart, full of joy, from me to you. It is a brain dump of what I think will be a very beneficial work for you guys.

As of the time of writing this preface, I did not pick a title of this book. And I'm feeling good about this. I know the topic and I can imagine how the book will look like. However, I feel that picking a title will force my thoughts through a narrow path and thus limit the potential of what this book could be. Obviously, if you are reading this that means I have already picked a title.

This book is about building web maps using Javascript technology. I picked Javascript because it is a resilient light-weight technology that can run on both the server and the client, mobile, IOT and supercomputer machines.

Traditional technology books discuss tools. "This is how to load a web map in a browser". "This is how to query the rest endpoint". "This is how to render a 3d map". You get a catalog of tools and what they do. There is nothing wrong with this format. In fact, it is a good reference. However, you don't get any context when reading such books to take action and build something. It is like learning what is a hammer, nail and screwdriver does but these tools are useless if no one shows you how to build a table using these tools.

I like to write my books by example, where I build an app and in the process explain the various tools I'm planning to use to build this app. Personally, I feel this is a better way of learning as it gives context.

I hope you enjoy this book.

What are we building?

We will be building a web mapping application from scratch. For tourists, we are building an app that helps users locate landmarks. The app shows the landmarks in a map such as libraries, cafes, restaurants schools and much more. It has a search capability to search for landmarks where they will be highlighted on the map. It also shows the nearby landmarks within specific miles from current location. So you can answer interesting questions such as show me all libraries within 100 feet of this coffee shop or are there any liquor stores within a mile from this school? I will be providing you with the sample data which I created myself, this data is not real it is just sample. All we need is to write the application. The app will run on both mobile and desktop.

Don't worry if this seems like a lot. We will break down those functionalities into different chapters and slowly walk through each.

Who this book is written for?

Anyone interested in learning how to build a web mapping application. Basic programming knowledge is recommended but not required. I will explain all that is required as we go through the book.

System Requirements

I designed this book in a way so you don't require a special or license to get started. I will be using a mac in this book but will include instructions for Windows and Linux. We will use ArcGIS Online free account to host our landmark data and ArcGIS Javascript API 4.x to write the web application. I will provide that data in GeoJSON format so we can upload it to ArcGIS Online. You can download the data from this link http://bit.ly/geojson-landmarks

Software Requirements

All you need on your machine is a text editor to write code and a web server to serve the static files. I will be using Node JS as a web server and Visual Studio Code as the text editor. We will take care of the download and installation of those two in chapter 1.

Enjoy the book and thank you for picking up the book.

Hussein Nasser

Chapter 1 - Getting Started

We will immediately dive in practical, another reason why I went solo on this book. Most book publishers force authors to write lengthy unnecessary introduction chapters to make their books look bigger. By the end of this chapter you will have a fully functional web app (no GIS work yet but that is coming). Since our web map application will be built on the web, we need to do some necessary setup steps to configure the web environment on your machine. This chapter will include the necessary setup required to start authoring a web app (an app on the web).

To run an app on the web you need to set up a web server. The web server serves your app to the browser. We will also learn what text editor to use to write the code for the app depending on whether you are on Windows, Mac or Linux. We start by explaining what a web server is, how to set up one in your preferred environment, write your first hello world web app and consume it from your computer and phone!

Here are some quick links for you to jump through this chapter.

- What is a Web Server?
- Setup the Web Server
    - NodeJS (Mac)
    - NodeJS (Windows)
    - NodeJS (Linux)
    - IIS (Windows)
- Download Your Text Editor
- Configure Web Server (Node JS only)
- Write your first Web App!
    - Basic HTML
    - Javascript

What is a Web Server?

A web server is a software that serves web content through the HTTP protocol. Any site you request through your browser is hosted on a remote web server and the communication is maintained via the HTTP protocol. The end result is mostly a web page on a form of HTML on your browser. Some backend code executions might happen as a result of the request for example authentication or querying a database. The result from the server can be served as something other than HTML, such as JSON, binary downloadable file, a JPEG image or much more.

A web server can serve static files like HTML, Javascript and CSS files which will be rendered and executed on the client, the browser in this case. It can also host code that can be executed on the server as a result of a request and return a result. Popular examples are REST APIs that can be written in Javascript through Node JS, Ruby, PHP, ASP.NET and many others programming languages. In this book, most of our work will execute client side through HTML and Javascript. We will build a web server to serve us those files.

Whatever we are building in this book will eventually live in a web server to be served to people requesting it. But first! We will turn your computer or laptop into a mini web server which can serve this work. Once that works, we know that it should work on any other machine or on the cloud.

There are many web servers that you can use to server static HTML/Javascript files. If you are on Windows easiest thing is to turn on IIS. If you are on mac NodeJs is your friend. I personally prefer NodeJS because its lightweight and can run on both Linux and Windows servers. Whatever code you will write can be served from both Linux and Windows machines and will be executed on the client.

Let's get started!

Setup the Web Server

Based on your environment we will set up the correct web server, I'll include all the environments just in case you want to experience on multiple ones. Once you set up your web server feel free to jump to the Download Text Editor section.

Node JS - Mac

Head to nodejs.org and download the LTS Mac version of **nodejs**. The current version at the time of writing this book is 8.12.0 LTS but shouldn't be a big difference if you have a newer version, send me a message on @hnasr on twitter if you run into trouble with a newer version. I respond quickly.

Install the Node JS through the normal setup process. Mac sure that both **nodejs** and **npm** are installed.

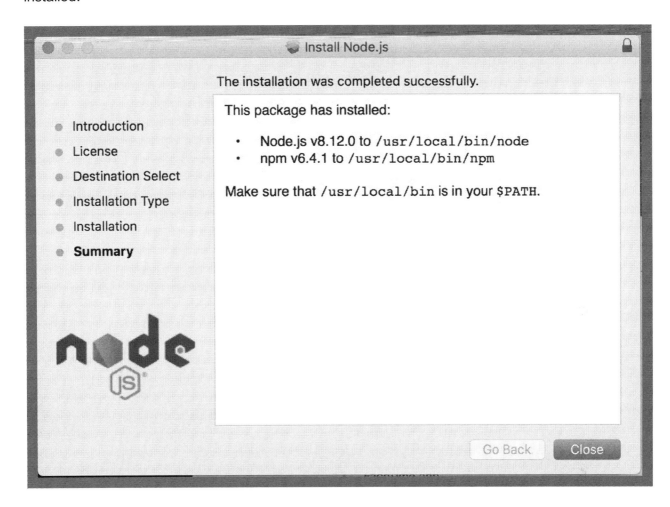

Test to make sure it works, open your terminal in mac and type in the following command. This should return the current version of node. Yours might have a different number but that's ok.

```
> node --version
```

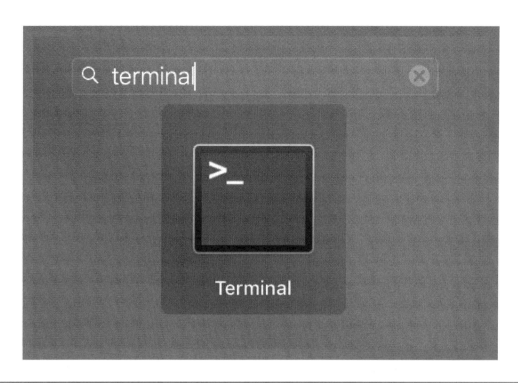

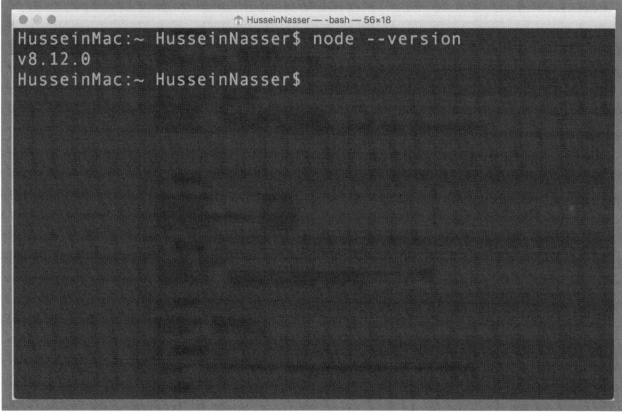

Node JS - Windows

Head to nodejs.org and download the LTS Windows version of nodejs. The current version while writing this book is 8.12.0 LTS but shouldn't matter if you have a newer version, send me a message on @hnasr on twitter if you run into trouble with a newer version.

Install the Node JS through the normal setup process, accept all defaults.

Test to make sure it works, open your command prompt (type in cmd in run) on Windows and type in the following command. This should return the current version of node. Yours might have a different number but that's ok.

> node --version

Node JS - Linux

To install Node JS on Ubuntu or any Debian Linux, we will need to add some distributions to the repro. On your Debian Linux box, open the terminal or ssh to the machine. I'm using my raspberrypi for this. Unfortunately, in Debian the command "node" is reserved by some other app, so unlike other operating systems, we will have to install it and execute it using nodejs command instead of just node. Write the following commands to install nodejs and npm into your box. You may get prompted to install, say yes.

```
curl -sL https://deb.nodesource.com/setup_8.x | sudo -E bash -
sudo apt-get update
sudo apt-get install nodejs
sudo apt-get install npm
```

Once you have run all the 4 commands, type in the following command

```
> nodejs --version
```

```
pi@raspberrypi:~ $ nodejs --version
v8.12.0
pi@raspberrypi:~ $
```

IIS - Windows

If you can see the folder *c:\inetpub\wwwroot* you are good to go! If not then you can turn IIS (Internet Information Services) from Windows features. From control panel, click on **Programs**. Then click on **Turn Windows features on or off.**

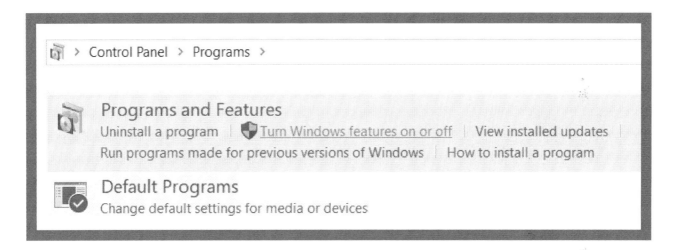

From the **Windows Features** dialog, make sure to check **Internet Information Services** and the **Web Management Tools**. Click **OK** to install.

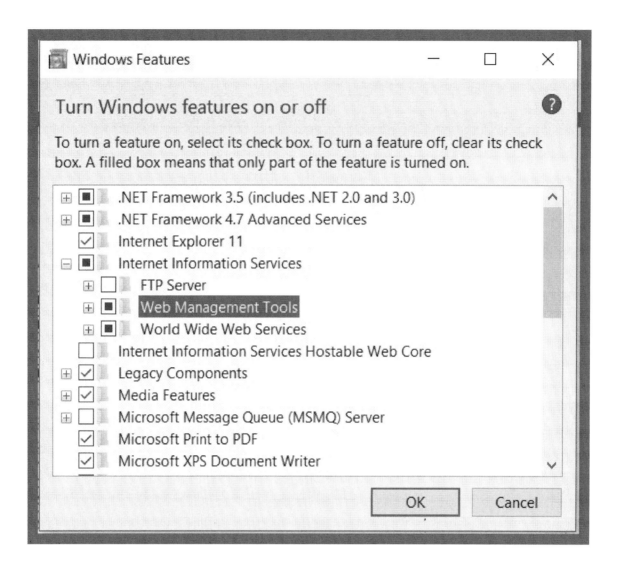

Once installed, test by visiting the page http://localhost/ or http://machinename. Where **machinename** is the hostname of the machine you installed IIS on. You should see the IIS welcome page. IIS listens on port 80, which is the default HTTP server port. That is why we don't have to add any port at the end of the URL because it is implied.

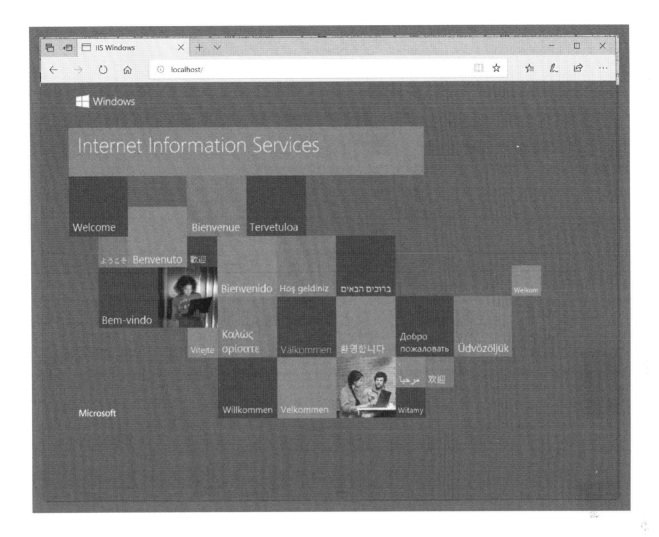

Download Text Editor

No matter what web server you picked, you are now ready to start coding. However, before we start we need a text editor to write our code with. The good thing about what we are building is that we only need a text editor, it doesn't require compiling or special interactive development environment (IDE). Use notepad or VIM or anything that you can write HTML / Javascript in. It can, however, become challenging as the code get big, that is why a good text editor helps.

In this book I will be using Visual Studio code, it has built-in syntax highlighting for HTML/CSS and Javascript and IntelliSense for Javascript which is pretty cool! It is available for both Windows, Mac and Linux. You can download it from code.visualstudio.com

Configure Web Server

If you have Windows and you decided to use IIS go ahead and skip to the next section Write your first Web app.

In this section, we will write a few lines of code in Node JS to configure the web server to serve static pages. Open your terminal and let's get started!

Note: If you prefer you can watch a video that I created about how to spin up a web server. http://bit.ly/nodewebserver then skip to the Write your first Web App section

From your terminal, navigate to any directory you want, and create a new folder called "hello" using **mkdir**. This will be your project folder.

```
HusseinMac:webapps HusseinNasser$ mkdir hello
HusseinMac:webapps HusseinNasser$ cd hello
HusseinMac:hello HusseinNasser$ ls -l
HusseinMac:hello HusseinNasser$ 
```

Once you are in the **hello** folder, type in

```
> npm init
```

Accept the defaults by hitting enter for everything but the test command. For the test command, write this instead **"node ."** You would want to write **"nodejs ."** if you are on Linux.

```
About to write to /Users/HusseinNasser/webapps/hello/package.json:

{
  "name": "hello",
  "version": "1.0.0",
  "description": "",
  "main": "index.js",
  "scripts": {
    "test": "node ."
  },
  "author": "",
  "license": "ISC"
}

Is this OK? (yes)
```

This will create **package.json** file which will be our node configuration we will use it to run node. Don't worry if you accidentally wrote this file, you can always edit that file manually and change the script. Notice that the file is expecting index.js file which doesn't exist. We need to create the index.js next.

Open Visual Studio code or your favorite text editor, from the File menu, select **Open** (or **Open Folder** in Windows) and browse to your **hello** folder.

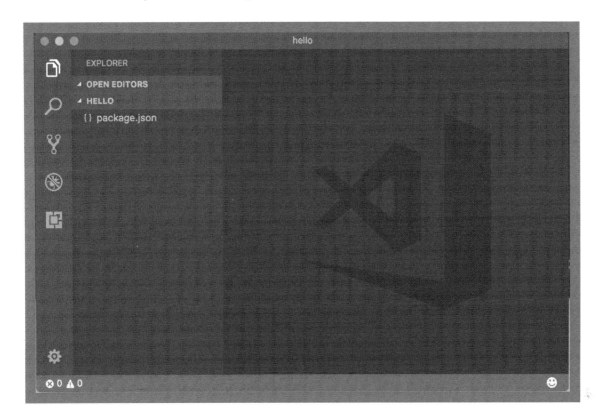

Create index.js by hovering over the **HELLO** folder section and click on **New File**. The **index.js** file will be executed on the server.

We will be using Express to set up the web server and listen on port 8080 where the traffic will be directed. To do that write the following code in your **index.js** file.

```
const app = require("express")();
```

This defines your Express application, and create a new instance of the application. We will use this app object to create an "endpoint" for your users to hit next. This is how you define an endpoint.

```
app.get("/hello", (req, res) =>
        res.send("Hello! This is my first web app"));
```

We used the app object to create an endpoint on /hello. This means if someone visited your web server http://machinename:port/hello we will return **"Hello, This is my first web app"** to the user. The last step is to listen on the port and start accepting HTTP requests.

```
app.listen(8080, () => console.log("Listening on port 8080"));
```

We used the app object again to start listening on port 8080 and when that is successful we will print the message "Listening on port 8080". This is for us only to make sure that the web server started successfully, the user won't see that.

Let's run the app. Save your work and go back to your terminal, make sure you navigate back to your hello folder. Then run this command

> npm test

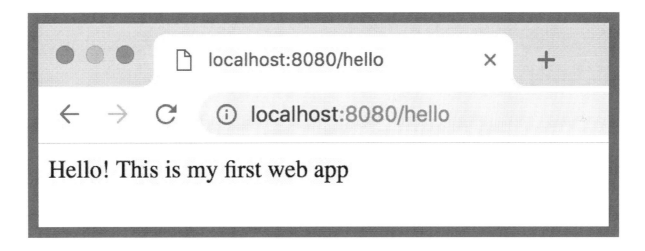

If you are seeing Listening on Port 8080 that means your web server is up and running. Let's put it to the test. Let's open a browser and navigate to http://localhost:8080/hello

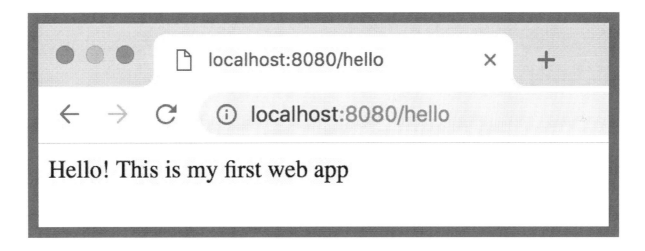

You can replace localhost with your machine name, You can find out your machine name by typing **hostname** in your terminal.

We just verified that our web environment is ready! Let's write some code. Save your work and close Visual Studio Code.

Here is the source code for this part

https://github.com/hnasr/gisprogrammingbook/tree/ch1-1

P.s. You can kill your web server by closing the terminal window or hitting CTRL+C on the terminal window which will terminate the web server app.

Write your first Web App

We will now write our first HTML code to test our web environment setup. If you are using IIS create a folder under c:\inetpub\www\ and call it "hello". This will be your web environment folder. Open **Visual Studio Code** or your favorite text editor. From the **File** menu, click **Open** (or **Open Folder** in mac) and navigate to your web environment folder, where your **hello** folder is located.

Basic HTML

Now create the **index.html** which will have most of our code. The **index.html** file will be executed on the client (browser).

In **Index.html** file, write the code that you want the user to see. Here is some HTML code.

```html
<html>
    <body><h1>Hello! My first web app</h1></body>
</html>
```

If you are using Windows IIS, simply navigate to http://localhost/hello and you should immediately see your page. If you are using Node JS, we need to make one small change to your **index.js** to start serving your **index.html** back to the user. Let's do that!

In your **index.js** replace res.send with res.sendFile and specify the index.html path as follows.

```js
app.get("/hello", (req, res) =>
    res.sendFile(__dirname + "/index.html"));
```

Let's run your code by going to http://localhost:8080/hello, notice that the font is a little bigger now because we used the h1 tag.

Here is the source code for this part

https://github.com/hnasr/gisprogrammingbook/tree/ch1-2

Javascript

Let's add some interactive elements to our basic **index.html** page using Javascript. This will prepare us to the next chapter. We will create a button and when the user clicks on this button we want to show an alert box welcoming the user to our web page. Let's start with the HTML code for the button. Here it is, noticed that we gave this button an id "**mybutton**", this is optional but we added that because we want to use it later.

```
<html>
    <body>
        <h1>Hello! My first web app</h1>
        <button id = 'mybutton'>Click me!</button>
    </body>
</html>
```

Let's try our web app, type http://localhost:8080/hello on your web browser, we can now see the button but nothing seems to happen when I click on it.

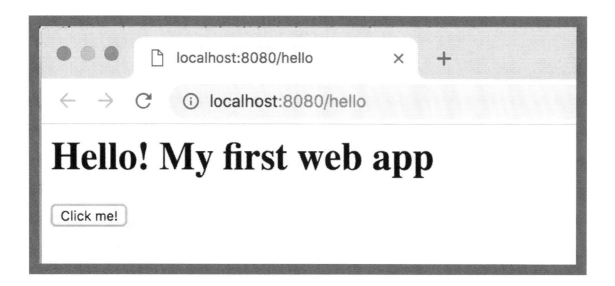

Let us add some logic to this button so that when someone clicks on it we want to show an alert. Write the following javascript code.

```html
<html>
    <body>
        <h1>Hello! My first web app</h1>
        <button id = 'mybutton'>Click me!</button>
        <script>
            const b = document.getElementById("mybutton");
            b.addEventListener("click", e => alert("You clicked me!"))
        </script>
    </body>
</html>
```

We first retrieved the button by using its Id "**mybutton**", then we added an event listener so that when someone clicks on it we execute the function **e => alert("You clicked me!")** where e is the event. Let's see if this works.

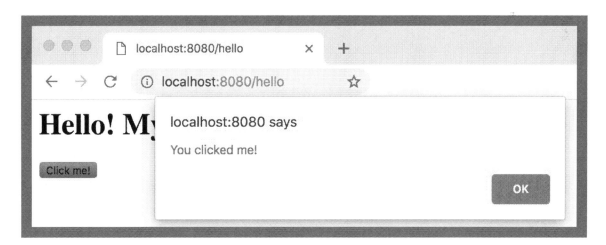

Source code for this part
https://github.com/hnasr/gisprogrammingbook/tree/ch1-3

P.S. If your phone and computer (where your web server is) are connected to the same WIFI connection you can open your phone browser and navigate to the web server http://machinename:8080/hello or http://machinename/hello if you are using IIS to execute your web app.

We have set up our web environment let us jump to some GIS programming.

Summary

In this chapter, we have successfully set up a web environment on Mac, Windows, and Linux which we can use to write all sort of web apps. During that, we learned what a web server is, configured one from scratch and listened on an HTTP port. We have also written some server-side code to serve HTML files to the client using Node JS and executed that by navigating to the end point we configured. We finally added some interactive elements on our web app with some javascript.

Now that we have our web environment ready, we can move to chapter 2 where we can start some GIS programming!

Chapter 2: Publishing the Sample Data and Web Map

I write all my books by example. That means I pick a project and build it throughout the chapters from scratch learning tools along the way. I find teaching by example approach more effective than teaching by tools. The project we picked for this book is a Landmark locator for the City of San Diego. The sample data in GeoJSON format is provided with this book for a small part of San Diego, we want to build a web application that visualizes the landmarks with good symbols, have a legend, ability to search for a landmark by name and type. Finally, the ability to do an area search to answer interesting questions such are there any liquor stores within a mile of a given school? Or where is the nearest hospital from an accident?

Note: The data provided with this book is completely fictitious and the landmarks don't exist in real life.

To build the application, we will first need to host the data on the cloud so we can consume it through the web app. Since what we are building is a client-side app, we will need to communicate with a server that has the data. That is why we will use ArcGIS Online to host the data and consume it from the web app that we will be building. ArcGIS Online is a rich Software as a Service that Esri offers to host data, perform rich analysis, mash up different layers and so much more. Esri offers a trial of ArcGIS Online for 21 days which we will be using in this book to host our data and write our app!

- Sign Up for ArcGIS Online
- What is a Feature Service?
- Publish to ArcGIS Online
- Enable Editing, Tracking and Attachment
- Create Web Map
- Making the Web Map Pretty
- Summary

Sign Up for ArcGIS Online

ArcGIS Online is based on the concept of organization. You can either join an existing organization (this could be your company) or create one from scratch and that is what we will be doing in this chapter. We will create an ArcGIS Online organization, we can do that with a free 21-day trial license. Let's get started.

Head over to esri.com/trial and fill in your details. The most important piece here is the company name this will become your organization name. Click on **Start Trial**.

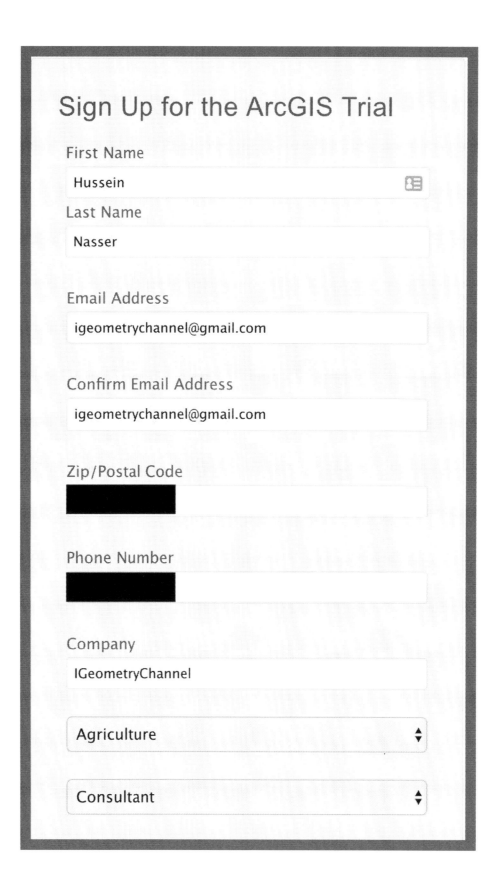

You will receive an email with your subscription id, and a link to activate your account click on the link.

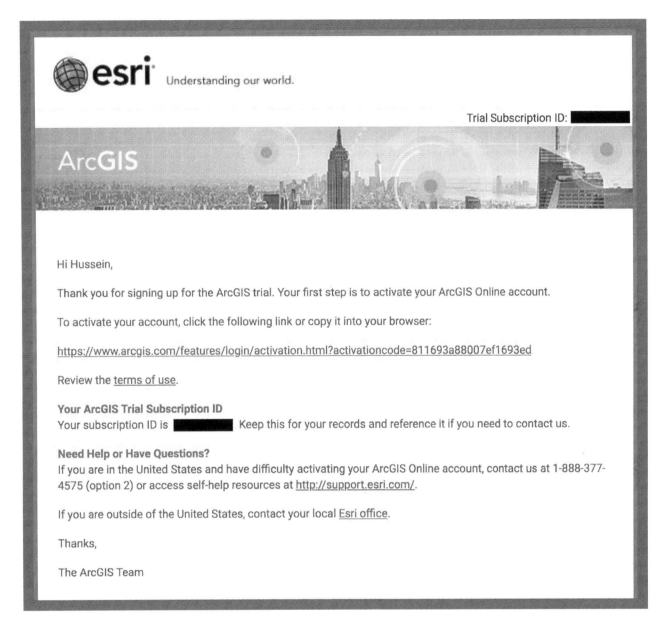

Your account will be active and you will be directed to your organization settings. You can give your organization a name, this will be present on your ArcGIS Online home page. You can give your organization a short name which will be used for your permanent URL. For instance, if your short organization name is **sanmark**, your ArcGIS Online URL will be https://**sanmark.maps.arcgis.com** and we will use this URL to access items from Javascript API and other web maps! So choose wisely and remember it well, because you will use it to log in. You can pick a default language for your org or let it default to whatever the browser is.

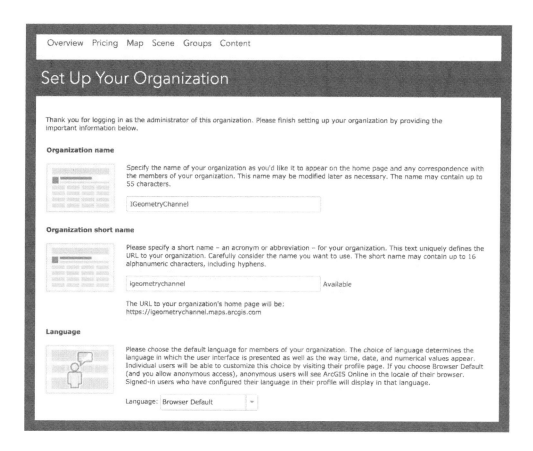

You can choose to set a region to personalize your experience and get maps related to your region. Finally, click **Save and Continue**.

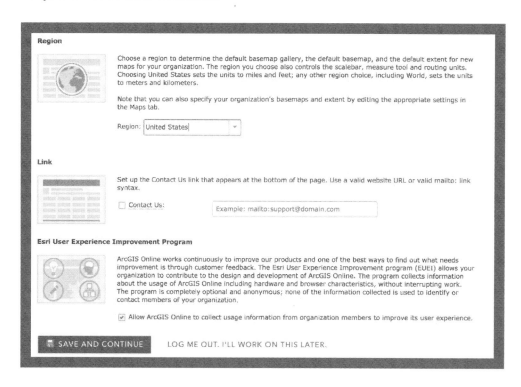

You will get a message welcoming you to ArcGIS Online and a prompt to either download ArcGIS desktop or continue with ArcGIS Online. If you are interested in learning more about Pro I recommend downloading it and watch the free series I did on ArcGIS Pro on IGeometry youtube channel. But you can do that on some other time, for now, click on **continue with ArcGIS Online**.

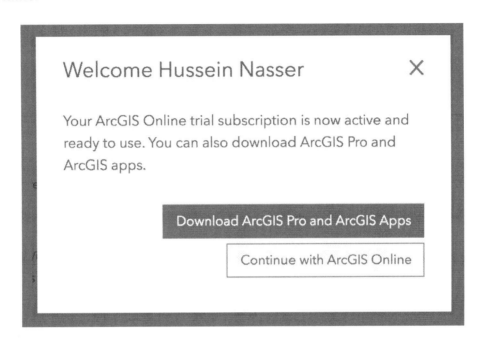

This means you are ready to start using the full capabilities of ArcGIS online, including the most important one for us, hosting a feature service. To come back to this page again open a browser and type in your URL, mine is https://igeometrychannel.maps.arcgis.com yours will be https://shortorgname.maps.arcgis.com then log in with the username that you activated.

What is a Feature Service?

There are several types of web mapping services offered by ArcGIS platform. The popular ones are Map service and feature service. Difference between the two is simple. When a client makes a request to a map service the server returns an image which is rendered quickly in the client side. While if the client makes a request to a feature service the client gets back "features" which are rows of the requested extent. Map service is for quick visualization of an extent without interactive options, while feature service is used to get finer details about the features themselves and interact with those features (editing for example). For example, if you want to simply view all restaurants in a given block without any interactivity you can use a map service but if you want to build a more engaging application you will need to use a feature service. That is what we will do in this chapter. We will upload our landmarks GeoJSON sample data which is available with this book (click here to download), which will create the feature service and a corresponding hosted feature layer on ArcGIS online. We will then consume the hosted feature layer in our Javascript web app.

Publishing to ArcGIS Online

In this section, we will take the **Landmarks.geojson** data provided with this book and publish it as a feature service. Head to your organization URL **https://igeometrychannel.maps.arcgis.com** and sign in with your account. Remember your URL is different than mine. Go back to Sign Up for ArcGIS Online section to learn more.

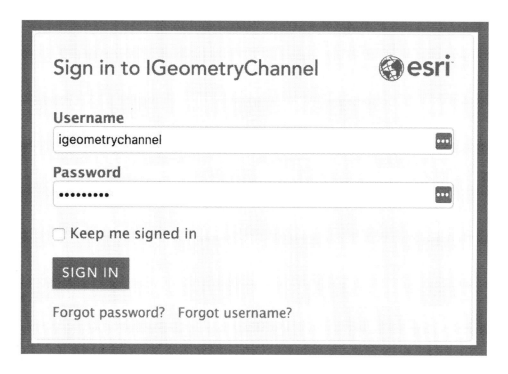

Once you sign in successfully you should see your organization home page. Click on **Content**.

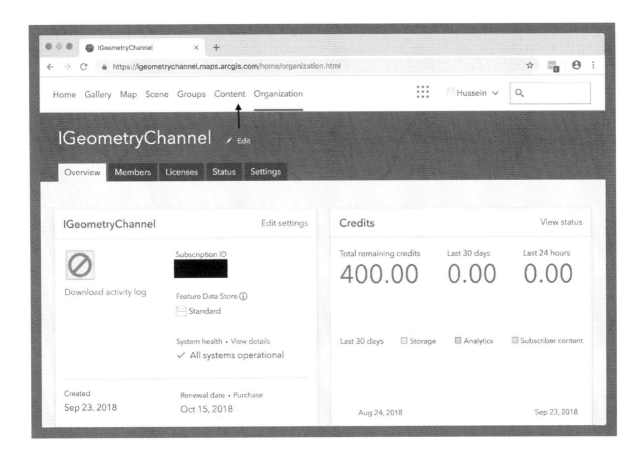

From **Add Item** menu, click on **From my computer**.

From the **Add an item from my computer** dialog, browse to the **landmarks.geojson** file which you have is part of the book data. You can download the sample data from here http://bit.ly/geojson-landmarks . Make sure to check the option to **Publish this file as a hosted layer,** this will create a feature service from our data. Write Landmarks as the **Title** and some **tags** as Illustrated below. Click **Add Item**.

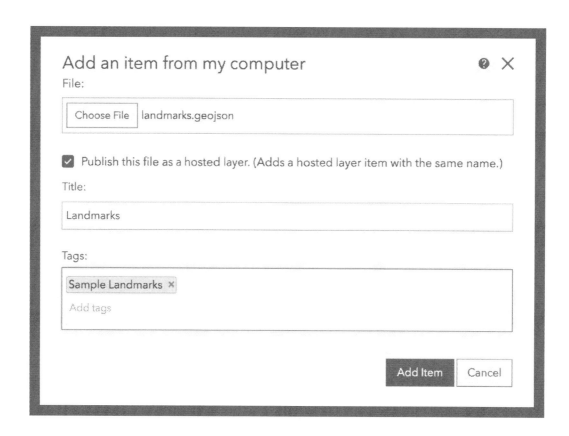

P.s. If you don't see the **Publish this file as a hosted layer checkbox option** this probably means that you did not activate ArcGIS trial that gives you these features.

Once your data is uploaded you will be directed to the feature layer to see its details. Few things happened here and let's try to explain. The **Landmarks.geojson** file is uploaded to ArcGIS Online, the data is then copied to the ArcGIS data store finally a feature service is created which points to the hosted datastore.

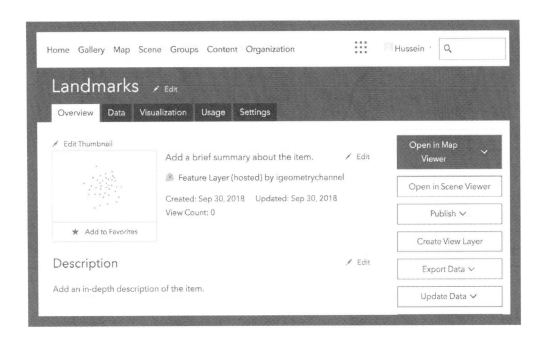

This is the hosted feature layer item that is hosted by ArcGIS Online. You can edit the thumbnail of this layer, description and configure different settings as we will see later. The feature layer points to the feature service we discussed earlier in the previous section. If you scroll down you will see that a layer is in your feature layer and a link to the feature service on ArcGIS Server.

Click on **Service URL** of the **Landmarks_0** layer (You might have different layer name) to open the Feature Service in **ArcGIS Server REST API**. You can immediately see interesting properties of this layer like the geometry type, scaling and much more.

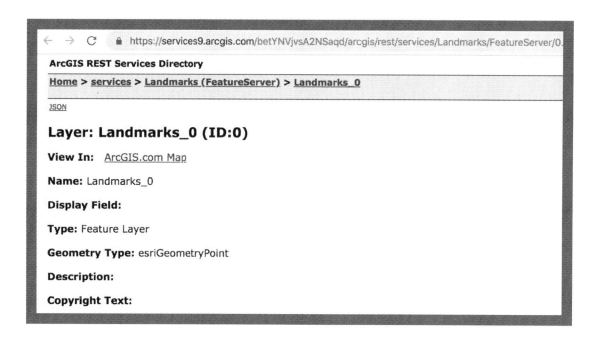

This is not all details on the feature service, there are far more details and you can get all of it by clicking on the JSON label on the top left. Every single property mean something, however, this is outside the scope of this book. I'm planning to write another book to just dive deep into the feature service.

```
"supportsValidateSql": true,
"supportsCoordinatesQuantization": true,
"supportsQuantizationEditMode": true,
"supportsApplyEditsWithGlobalIds": false,
"advancedQueryCapabilities": { … }, // 19 items
"useStandardizedQueries": true,
"geometryType": "esriGeometryPoint",
"minScale": 144448,
"maxScale": 0,
"extent": { … }, // 5 items
"drawingInfo": { … }, // 1 item
"allowGeometryUpdates": true,
"hasAttachments": false,
"htmlPopupType": "esriServerHTMLPopupTypeNone",
"hasM": false,
"hasZ": false,
"objectIdField": "ObjectId",
"uniqueIdField": { … }, // 2 items
"globalIdField": "",
"typeIdField": "",
"fields": [
    {
        "name": "marker_color",
        "type": "esriFieldTypeString",
        "actualType": "nvarchar",
        "alias": "marker-color",
        "sqlType": "sqlTypeNVarchar",
        "length": 256,
        "nullable": true,
        "editable": true,
        "domain": null,
        "defaultValue": null
    },
```

NOTE: The Feature Service lives in an ArcGIS Server instance, learn more about ArcGIS Server by watching this playlist on my youtube videos or check out my book.
www.husseinnasser.com/books

Let's summarize what happened during publishing in a diagram, you uploaded the file geodatabase to your organization. The GeoJSON file was uploaded successfully as an item to your organization, but because you chose the option to publish a hosted feature layer, the data was also copied to a back-end database, then a feature service on an ArcGIS Server was created pointing to the data on the database, then a feature layer item was created on your organization.

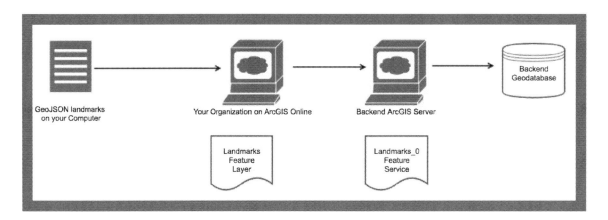

To learn more about Geodatabase take a look at my book Learning ArcGIS Geodatabases or you can follow me on my podcast (anchor.fm/hnasr) or YouTube (youtube.com/igeometry) channel where I talk I explain about this technology.

Enable Editing, Tracking, and Attachments

Multi-User editing is one of the capabilities that we can enable on a feature service, concurrency atomicity isolation and durability (ACID) are handled by the back-end datastore that ArcGIS Online. While multiple users are making edits to your service, you want to track of when an edit was made and which user created or updated a **feature**. Another capability is attachments, which allows you to upload files and attach them to a feature, an example will be an image of a restaurant.

Feature: Feature is a row in a table with a shape field that defines its geometry.

To Learn more about ACID
https://www.youtube.com/playlist?list=PLQnIjOFTspQXBzVO0w5uzmclAUwgOhdt1

Editing, tracking, and Attachments can be enabled from the settings page on the feature service. Let us enable those on our feature service. Make sure your organization homepage is opened and click on the **Contents** tab. You should see your **Landmarks** Feature Layer (Hosted) and the GeoJSON file that you uploaded as illustrated below.

Click on the **Landmarks** Feature Layer (hosted), then click on **Settings**

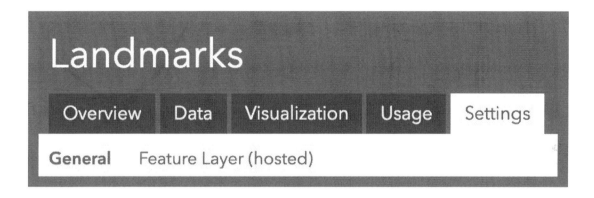

Scroll down Feature layer (hosted) section, make sure **Keep Editing**, **Keep track of created and updated features** and **Keep track of who created and last updated features** options are checked.

Feature Layer (hosted)

Editing

☑ Enable editing.

☑ Keep track of created and updated features.

☑ Keep track of who created and last updated features.

☐ Enable Sync (disconnected editing with synchronization).

With Feature Layer you have fine grain control on what users can edit, what users can see what and so on. We won't be using these options in this book but feel free to experiment! For now, Click **Save** to persist your chances.

Create Web Map

We have the back-end infrastructure ready to go, we need to start working on what our app will actually consume and see. The web map.

Web maps are maps that are authored by mashing up one or more layers to solve interesting visualization challenges, discover new patterns, quickly identify an anomaly and much more. They are called web maps because they can be consumed via the web using the HTTP protocol. Each layer in the web map can be rendered with different symbols, scale suppression, turn completely on and off and much more. Web Maps are easy to build in ArcGIS Online, in this section we will create one of our Landmarks feature layer.

Head to your organization home page https://shortorgname.maps.arcgis.com/, click on **Map.** this will open the Map Viewer with a brand new map.

Home   Gallery   Map   Scene   Groups   Content   Organization

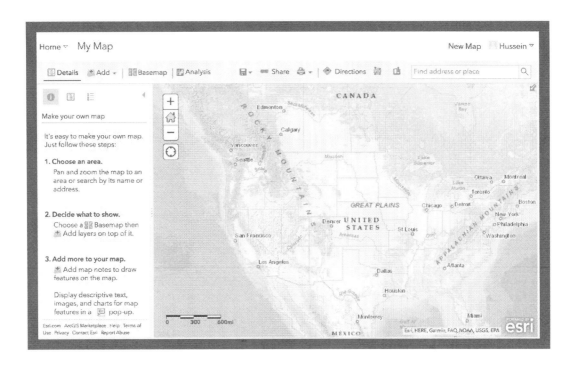

Next, we need to add our **Landmarks** feature layer to our new map. From the **Add** menu, click on Search for Layers which will retrieve your content.

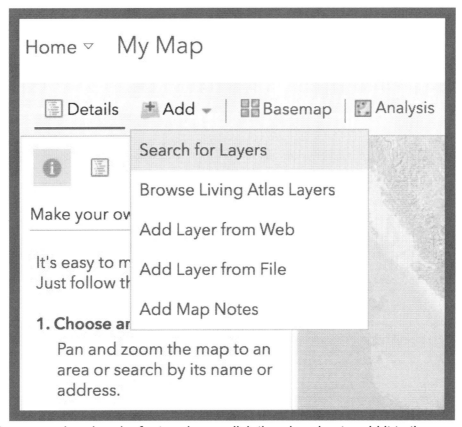

You should see your Landmarks feature layer, click the plus sign to add it to the map.

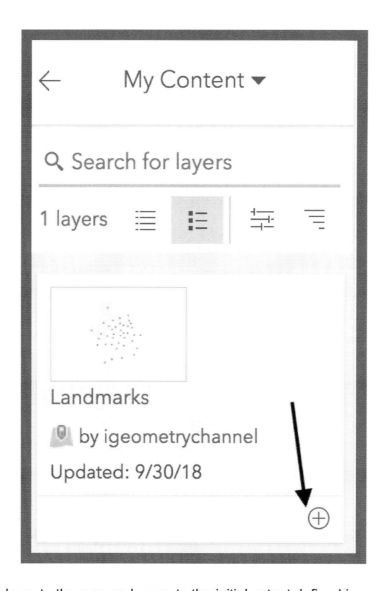

This will add your layer to the map and zoom to the initial extent defined in your layer.

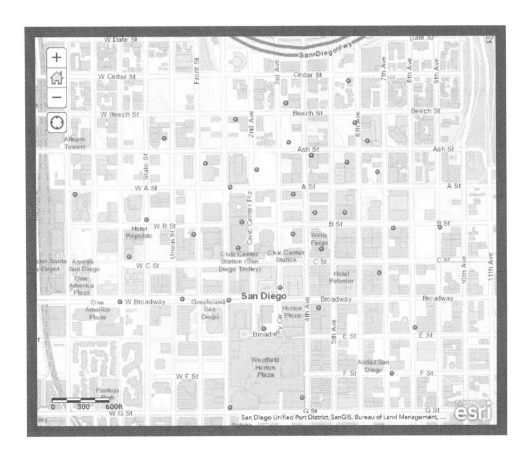

Save the map by clicking the on the **Save** icon and type in the name of the map and other details as illustrated below.

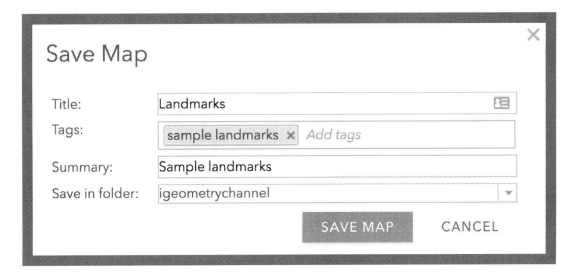

Go back to your **Contents** tab, you should now see your new web map created as a new item. Click on the **Landmarks** Web Map.

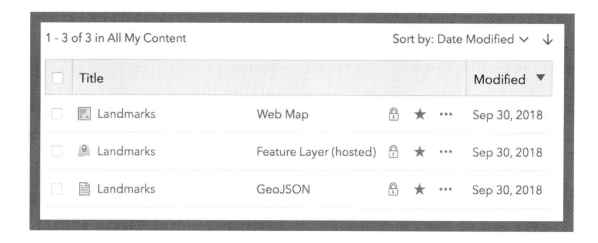

Each item in portal has an Item Id to uniquely identifies it. The item id is also used in the Javascript API to retrieve an item in ArcGIS Online. Our Web Map also has an item Id as illustrated in this picture.

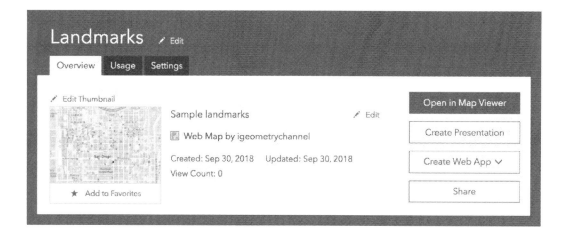

Making the Web Map Pretty

Since we will be consuming this map from our application, we need to make it little prettier by changing the symbols of the landmarks. In one of the layers in the uploaded data is called **Landmarks** there is a string field called **Type** which describes the type of the landmark whether it is a school or a restaurant etc. We want to render the layer based on the type of the landmark.

Open your **Landmarks Web Map** and from **Contents** pane, click on **Change Style**.

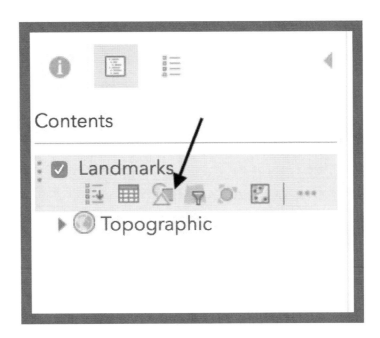

From the **Change Style** pane, in the Choose an attribute to show drop-down list, pick the **Type** field. In the **Drawing Style**, pick **Types (Unique Symbols)** as illustrated below.

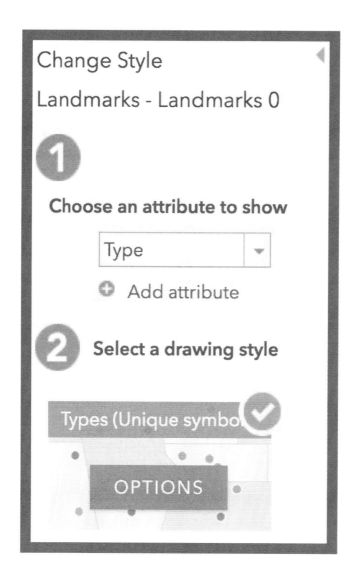

In the **Drawing Style**, click on **Options** to start defining the symbols. You should see the unique codes and how many corresponding features are in each category. For example, we can see we have 12 restaurants and 3 hospitals in the sample data.

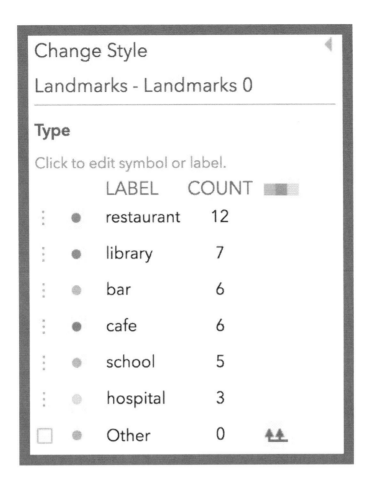

Optionally, start defining labels based on the provided category table and set a symbol for each category. You can do that by clicking on the symbol and choose from various symbols.

Here is an example of what I did.

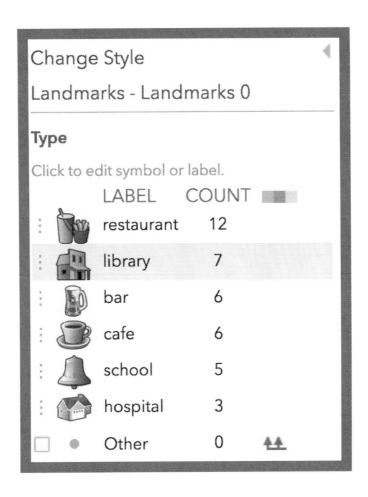

Click **Done** to persist your changes and then **Save** your map! Take pride in your work. Even without a single line of code, you have gone so far. Imagine what you can do when you actually add some programming magic to this?

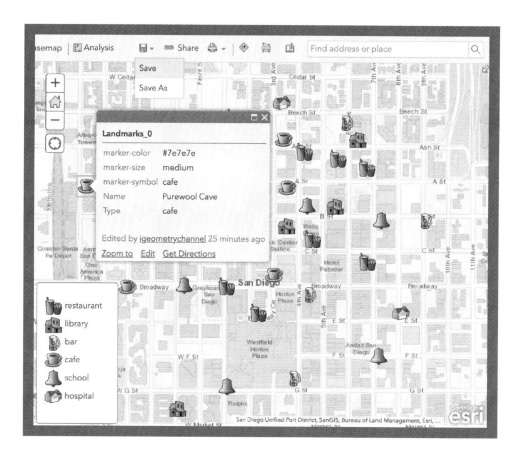

Summary

In this chapter, we have signed up for a free 21 days ArcGIS Online which will manage our gis data and maps. With this, we were able to upload our sample data to the cloud, create a feature layer and then created a web map. We learned about the data store, the feature service, feature layer, and the web map. We spent some time to build a good web map, added unique symbols to each landmark type so we can better visualize them in the map. In the next chapter, we will start consuming the web map we created and build our web application.

Chapter 3: Building the Web Application

This is the moment you all waiting for. We have our web server, we have our data hosted and a web map configured. All we need to do is write the application. This is what we will be doing in this chapter, brace yourselves this chapter is long and it has a lot of new abstractions. No worries though we will explain every single one of them along the way.

Here are some quick links for you to jump through this chapter.

Basic Javascript

Before we dive into GIS programming with Javascript, we need to learn a few key things about Javascript as a language. In this section, we will talk about JSON, objects, arrays, and promises.

JSON

JSON stands for Javascript object notation. I'll be honest, JSON was very confusing to me in the beginning. Coming from a background of strongly typed language where you have to define your variables types explicitly, it took me a while until I grasp it. It is really simple though once you get the gist of it.

Objects vs Arrays

Objects and arrays are the basic building blocks in JSON. Objects have curly braces while arrays have square brackets []. Objects can optionally have 1 or more key-value pairs the key is a string while the value could be anything including another object or an array. Here is an example of a movie JSON object, the movie JSON object has a **Title** key with a string value, it has **Year** key with an integer value, and it has a **Director** key with a JSON object as its value.

The movie object also has an **FAQ** key with a value as an array of strings representing the questions. It also has an **Actors** key with a value as an array of actor objects, each object has a name as a string and role as a string. Here is the movie object.

```javascript
let movie = {
        "title" : "The Shawshank Redemption",
        "year" : 1994,
        "director" : {
            "name": "Frank Darabont",
            "placeOfBirth": "Montbéliard, Doubs, France",
            "dateOfBirth": "January 28, 1959"
        },
        "faq" : [
            "Q: The movie is dedicated to an Allen Greene. Who was he?",
            "Q: What was Red's crime?",
            "Q: How faithful is the film to the original novella?"
        ],
        "actors" : [
            {
                "name" : "Tim Robbins",
                "role" : "Andy Dufresne",
            },
            {
                "name" : "Morgan Freeman",
                "role" : "Ellis Boyd 'Red' Redding",
            }
        ]
    }
```

Let us try to manipulate this object with javascript in preparation of what is coming next.

Working with JSON objects

In this section we will learn how to work and manipulate JSON objects, we will need these skills to proceed through GIS programming since we will be working with JSON objects a lot. Hope you still have the code from Chapter 1 handy because we will use it but just in case you don't here it is.

https://github.com/hnasr/gisprogrammingbook/tree/ch1-3

Open the **index.html** and add the movie object code right after script tag, make sure the rest of the code you already have goes below your object as follows. This will store the JSON object into a variable called **movie**.

```
<script>
let movie = {
        "title" : "The Shawshank Redemption",
        "year" : 1994,
        "director" : {
                "name": "Frank Darabont",
                "placeOfBirth": "Montbéliard, Doubs, France",
                "dateOfBirth": "January 28, 1959"
        },
        "faq" : [
                "Q: The movie is dedicated to an Allen Greene. Who
was he?",
                "Q: What was Red's crime?",
                "Q: How faithful is the film to the original
novella?"
        ],
        "actors" : [
                {
                        "name" : "Tim Robbins",
                        "role" : "Andy Dufresne",
                },
                {
```

```
                "name" : "Morgan Freeman",
                "role" : "Ellis Boyd 'Red' Redding",
            }
        ]
    }
        const b = document.getElementById("mybutton");
        b.addEventListener("click", e => alert("You clicked
me!"))
        </script>
```

Remember we have written some code to show an alert message "You clicked me!" when one clicks on **mybutton**. We can change that to show the title of the movie. This is how you do it.

```
...
        ]
    }
        const b = document.getElementById("mybutton");
        b.addEventListener("click", e => alert(movie.title))
        </script>
```

Let's save your work, run your server npm test then go to http://localhost:8080/hello click on the button, you should see the title of the movie.

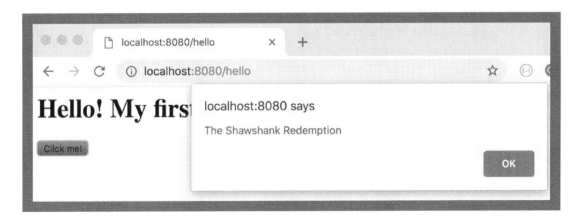

Let's augment the code to show more info. Like the year the movie aired, and the director name. The beauty of javascript is you can add a new line and continue writing your code normally.

```
b.addEventListener("click",
e => alert(movie.title + " " + movie.year + " " +
movie.director.name))
```

You can find the source code for this code for this section here

https://github.com/hnasr/gisprogrammingbook/tree/ch3-1

Okay, next we will do some more interesting stuff. let's show all the actors names and their roles in the movie. We were getting away with writing all of this in one line of code using the arrow function. But now we will have to add curly braces because we need to write multiple lines of code in our little function. So as a start just add curly braces indicating that we are about to write more than 1 line of code.

```
b.addEventListener("click",
    e => {
        alert(movie.title + " " + movie.year + " " +
movie.director.name)
    }
);
```

Since **actors** is an array in the movie object, we will loop through it using forEach. ForEach is a loop predicate that allows us to navigate each "element" in the array and do something with it. ForEach takes a function and will essentially call the function passing every element in the array. Let's do this.

```
b.addEventListener("click",
    e => {
            alert(movie.title + " " + movie.year + " " +
movie.director.name)
            movie.actors.forEach(a => alert(a.name))
    }
    );
```

Refresh your page, and click on the button you will see 3 alert boxes. The first showing the movie info and the two showing the actors.

You can find the latest source code here

https://github.com/hnasr/gisprogrammingbook/tree/ch3-2

I love this stuff and we can go multiple chapters just playing with JSON, I think this is enough so let's just move to the next section. Promises.

P.s. You can see Visual Studio Code show you IntelliSense so you don't have to think about the name of the objects.

```
e => {
    alert(movie.title + " " + movie.year +
    movie.a|
}                    actors  (property) "act... ⓘ
);                   addEventListener
                     alert
```

Understanding Promises

Promises are one of the recently introduced features in Javascript. It allows us to write non-blocking, asynchronous readable code that can deliver great user experience.

Here is an example of a Request method that calls a URL, downloads a text file. When the method succeeds, the promise is resolved and the "then" is called, when the method fails, the promise is rejected and "catch" is called instead. Here is an example.

```
Request("http://url/download.txt")
    .then(result => alert(result))
    .catch(err => alert("Error downloading file. " + err )
```

We will use promises a lot throughout this book.

ArcGIS Javascript API 4.9

The ArcGIS for Javascript API is a collection of APIs that Esri has developed to author web mapping applications. You can use the API to render and interact with web maps and create graphics. You can use it to render 2D and 3D maps, add layers, query features from feature services or map services, edit your features manipulate the symbology of your layers. Plus so many other options that are available.

Learn more about what this API can do here. https://developers.arcgis.com/javascript/
The latest release as of the writing of this book is 4.9, this book will use this version.

In 2017, I have started a YouTube tutorial series where we have built a map viewer from scratch using ArcGIS Javascript API 4.x. The series is very popular and I believe it will be beneficial to you. If you already purchased this book from this series, thank you very much for your support and I hope that you will learn more from this book.

Click here for the series
https://www.youtube.com/watch?v=rft4ZecPQcl&list=PLQnljOFTspQUppK8iiluoQJTAj436IWQz

Loading the API

We will use the index.html file and delete all the code that we previously wrote. You can start a brand new project or continue using the "hello" project totally up to you. Feel free to back it up as another name if you want to keep it. Remember the source code is always on GitHub.

Delete all code in the index.html and type instead **html:5** and hit tab.

Once you hit tab, you should see some boilerplate HTML 5 code in preparation for our work. Remember this is only in Visual Studio Code, if you are using some other editor then simply write the code below.

```html
<!DOCTYPE html>
<html lang="en">
<head>
    <meta charset="UTF-8">
    <meta name="viewport" content="width=device-width, initial-scale=1.0">
    <meta http-equiv="X-UA-Compatible" content="ie=edge">
    <title>Document</title>
</head>
<body>
</body>
</html>
```

In the Head section, insert the necessary script below to reference the ArcGIS Javascript API 4.9 API. The first line is to link the styles and the second one is which contains the API. Also, change the title of the page. I chose **San Diego Landmark Locator.**

```html
.....
<head>
    <meta charset="UTF-8">
    <meta name="viewport" content="width=device-width, initial-scale=1.0">
    <meta http-equiv="X-UA-Compatible" content="ie=edge">
    <title>San Diego Landmark Locator</title>
    <link rel="stylesheet" href="https://js.arcgis.com/4.9/esri/css/main.css">
    <script src="https://js.arcgis.com/4.9/"></script>
</head>
.....
```

Run your app, npm test and navigate to http://localhost:8080/hello You should see an empty page with just a title. Next section we will start loading the map. This is no longer a hello world app, so maybe let's change the endpoint from /hello to just / so we can access the site by simply typing http://localhost:8080/. Do you remember where to change that? Correct **index.js**

```javascript
const app = require("express")();
app.get("/", (req, res) =>
```

```
          res.sendFile(__dirname + "/index.html"));
app.listen(8080, () => console.log("Listening on port 8080"));
```

Here is the source code for this section with all these changes.

https://github.com/hnasr/gisprogrammingbook/tree/ch3-3

The Map and the MapView

We will now add the basic building blocks to load a MapView and Map. MapView is the
container that will contain one or more maps, we load it into an HTML div element. The Map is
where all the layers and basemaps go. Let's go back to your **Index.html** and add the div HTML
element where the map should go. We will give it an id so we can uniquely identify it. We will
use this id in multiple places.

```
...
<body>
    <div id = 'divMapView'></div>
</body>
...
```

ArcGIS Javascript API has a lot of classes and by default, none of them are loaded, you only
load what you absolutely need. So we will load the MapView and the Map classes from the
ArcGIS javascript API so we can use them and render the topological basemap. To load the
classes we use the "**require**" function. Add a new script tag in your header tag right after your
Javascript API.

```
...
    <script src="https://js.arcgis.com/4.9/"></script>
    <script>
    </script>
</head>
<body>
...
```

Require is a function that takes two parameters. The first is an array of class names that you want to load as strings, and the second parameter is a function which takes parameters that those classes are passed to.

```
...
<script>
require ([],() => { /* do something */})
</script>
...
```

Here is an example where we are loading class1 and class2 into C1 and C2 parameters.

```
...
<script>
require (["class1", "class2"],(C1, C2) => { /* do something */})
</script>
...
```

The classes we want to load are "esri/Map", "esri/views/MapView" so let's load them. The order must match the order of the parameters in the function. I just added a new line to make the code more readable. /* do something */ is where most of our code will go.

```
...
<script>
require (["esri/views/MapView", "esri/Map"],
(MapView, Map) => {
    /* do something */
})
</script>
...
```

Next, we will create a map and load a sample basemap in it. We will then create a map view object, ask it to render into our div view element then load the map object in the map view.

We will create the map object in memory first. The Map class takes a JSON object with many parameters such as what basemap or layers you want to load this map with. We will load no layers yet, just the basemap and we will pick the topographic basemap.

You can find more details about the Map class here
https://developers.arcgis.com/javascript/latest/api-reference/esri-Map.html

```
...
    <script>
        require (["esri/Map", "esri/views/MapView"],
        ( Map , MapView ) => {
            const map = new Map({ "basemap": "topo"});
        })
    </script>
...
```

The map object we created is just in memory, we need to display it somewhere, and that will be in the MapView. The MapView also takes a JSON object with some parameters what we are interested in here is the container and guess what else? Yes, The map!

Find more about the MapView object here
https://developers.arcgis.com/javascript/latest/api-reference/esri-views-MapView.html

```
...
<script>
    require (["esri/Map", "esri/views/MapView"],
    (Map,MapView) => {
        const map = new Map({"basemap": "topo"});
        const mapView = new MapView({
            "container" : "divMapView",
            "map" : map
        })
    })
</script>
...
```

Save your work and npm test to start your web server and navigate to http://localhost:8080

Nothing! But no worries because we know why. The map view div element requires that you specify a width and height.

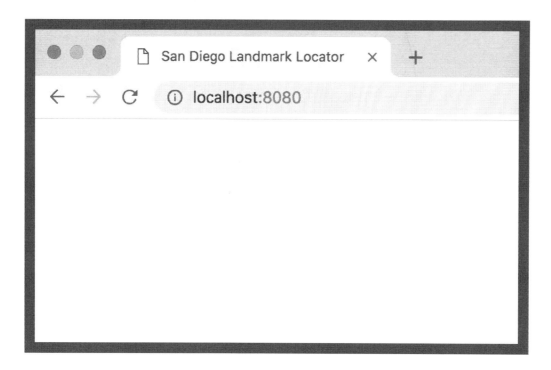

So let us specify some fixed height and width for the **divMapView** div element using a CSS style. In the head section of your HTML file add a style tag as following and make the map size 500 by 500 pixels.

```
. . .
<head>
    <meta charset="UTF-8">
    <meta name="viewport" content="width=device-width, initial-
scale=1.0">
    <meta http-equiv="X-UA-Compatible" content="ie=edge">
    <style>
    #divMapView {
        width:500px;
        height:500px;
    }
    </style>
    <title>San Diego Landmark Locator</title>
. . .
```

Save and head to http://localhost:8080, we can see the basemap finally. Good work.

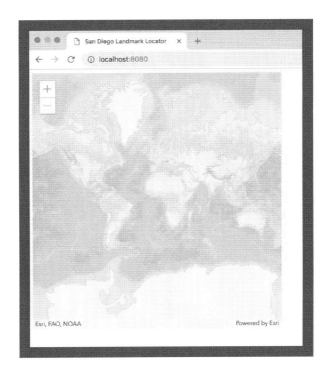

I think it will look even better when we put the map view as full screen and remove all padding on the sides.

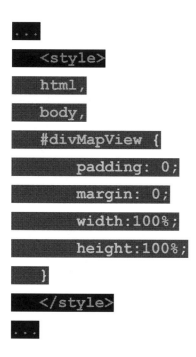

```
    . . .
    <style>
    html,
    body,
    #divMapView {
        padding: 0;
        margin: 0;
        width:100%;
        height:100%;
    }
    </style>
    . . .
```

You can use your mouse to zoom in and navigate the world and notice how we are in fullscreen mode.

I think we are ready to move to the next section where we will render the web map. Here is the source code for this section so you can check your work.

Loading Web Map from ArcGIS Online

In this section, we will render the web map that we have prepared in chapter 2 using the ArcGIS Javascript API. Then we will test our app and run it from both the computer and phone.

The Web Map Item

First, do you still remember your web map item id? It is ok if you don't, let's go to your ArcGIS Online page. Mine is https://igeometrychannel.maps.arcgis.com yours will be shortname.maps.arcgis.com. Once you log in, go to **Contents**. From the Contents list click on the 3 dots and then click View Item Details. You can also just click on the **Landmarks** Web Map.

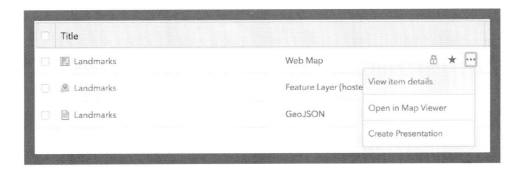

Once you open the item, take a closer look at the URL, you will see a unique set of string right after **?id=** that is your item id. Copy it and make it handy.

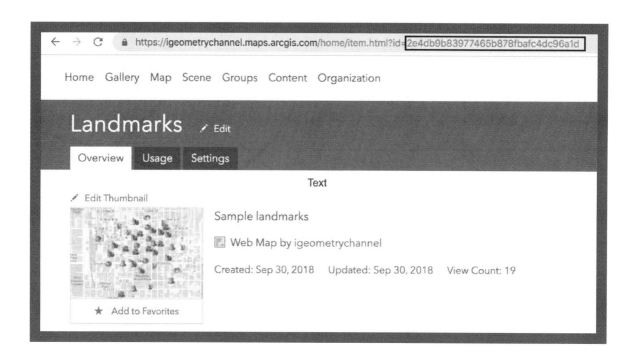

Back to the code! We will need to make very few minor changes to our code instead of loading a map we load a web map. That also means that we no longer need to load the Map class, and we will need to load the WebMap class, finally, we will remove the JSON object that we pass to the WebMap class.

Learn more about the WebMap class here
https://developers.arcgis.com/javascript/latest/api-reference/esri-WebMap.html

```
...
<script>
    require (["esri/WebMap", "esri/views/MapView"],
    (WebMap,MapView) => {
        const map = new WebMap({});
        const mapView = new MapView({
            "container" : "divMapView",
            "map" : map
        })
    })
</script>
...
```

We will then change the JSON Object that we pass to the WebMap to add the id of our WebMap. The **portalItem** is another JSON object that has id key.

```
...
<script>
    require (["esri/WebMap", "esri/views/MapView"],
    (WebMap,MapView) => {
        const map = new WebMap({
            "portalItem" : {
                "id" : "2e4db9b83977465b878fbafc4dc96a1d"
            }
        });
        const mapView = new MapView({
            "container" : "divMapView",
            "map" : map
        })
    })
</script>
...
```

Save your work, open command prompt and run **npm test** to start up your web server. Head to http://localhost:8080. You will notice that you get a prompt to enter your username and password. That makes sense since that is your web map which is secured so nobody can just get access to it, all of this is controlled by ArcGIS Online. Enter your credentials to log in.

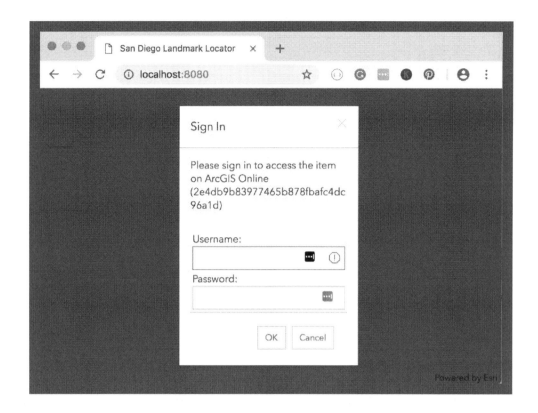

Once you login you should see your web map loaded into your web application.

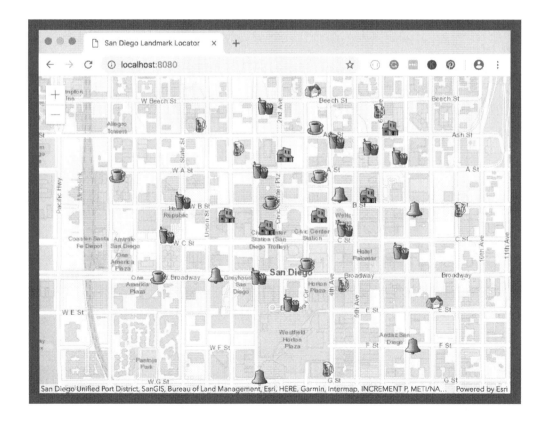

Web Map Security

If you don't want to get prompted you can make your WebMap public from your organization content page. If you are happy keeping your WebMap secure skip this section.

Click on the lock icon and check "**Everyone (public)**" then click **OK**.

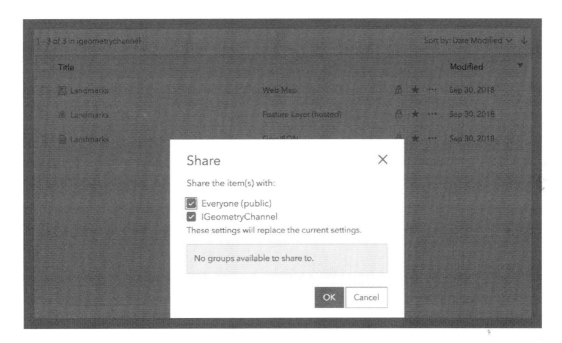

Sharing WebMap is not enough to make your web map public, because the WebMap turns around and pull the Feature Layer which is not shared publically yet. This prompt will let you share the feature layer Landmarks as well with the public. Click **Update Sharing**.

Note: Your organization might not allow sharing to the public.

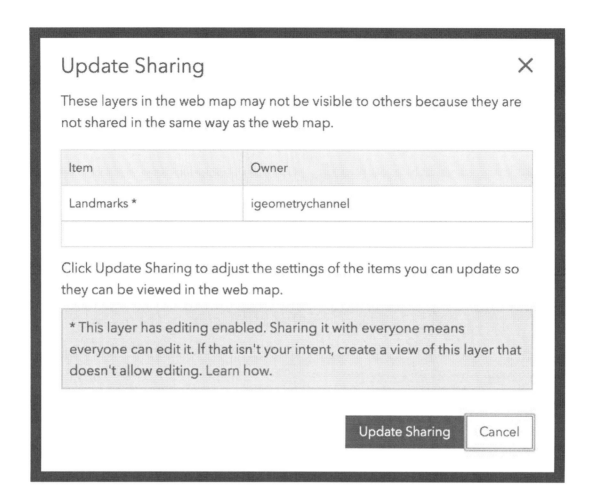

You will notice that the lock Icon on the Web Map and the Feature Layer is changed to a world icon indicating it has been shared publically. Again you don't have to do that if you want to keep your Service secure. You can also decide to share the service with certain members or groups too. That is the power of ArcGIS Online.

The ArcGIS Javascript API gives you some functionality out of the box, like navigation, control, and ability to identify features. Click on one of your landmarks.

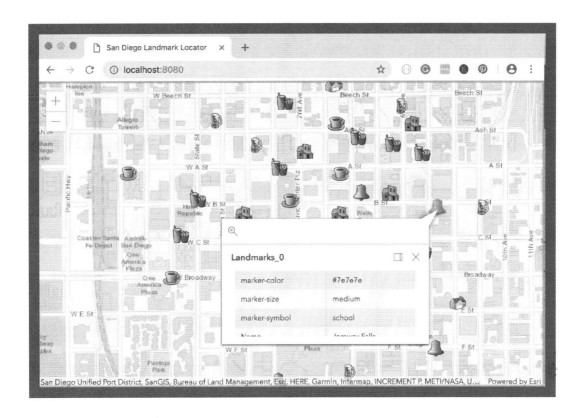

Viewing the Web Application from Smartphone or Tablet

The beauty of what you just built is not only you can access it from your machine, you can actually serve this app right now off your phone. This is because the ArcGIS Javascript API is mobile compatible. Give it a shot, take your Android, iPhone or even tablet and navigate to http://machinename:8080 where **machinename** is the name of the machine that you are running your web server on. Find out the name using command prompt by typing hostname

Here is a screenshot of the web application from my iPhone.

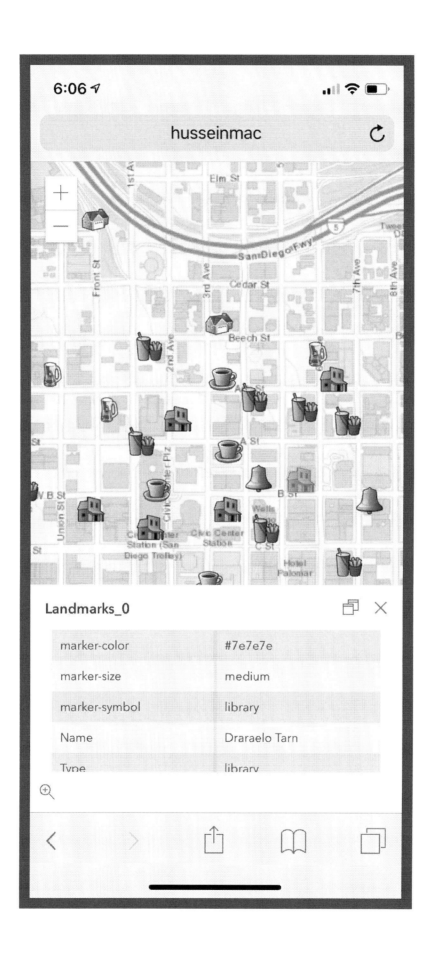

The final source code of our application can be found here
https://github.com/hnasr/gisprogrammingbook/tree/ch3-5

Summary

This was a very rich chapter. We learned the basics of Javascript, JSON objects and arrays and promises. We have introduced the ArcGIS Javascript API which allows building mapping applications using Javascript. We introduced the MapView, Map and the WebMap classes in the API. We also loaded the WebMap which we created in the previous chapter into our application and changed the security of the web map. Finally, we accessed the web mapping application from smartphone proving that the API is mobile compatible.

In the next chapter, we will write learn how to build the searching capability which will allow us to search and filter our landmarks. This will make our app more useful.

Chapter 4: Building Search Capability

Search is a key capability in almost any web application. Any user expects to find things quickly using search in the app so in this chapter we will show how to add different search capabilities in our applications.

Here are some quick links for you to jump through this chapter.

The Layer

A layer is a very important artifact in any geographic information system. It represents a collection of features (rows in the underlying table) that share the same shape. Because I come from a relational database background, I like to think of a layer as a table in the database with a shape column. Layers can also be configured with different symbologies, scale suppression, custom definition queries. If you remember we rendered the Landmarks layer that we published in Chapter 2 on its type field. The layer can be used as a resource to query the features in it and that is what we will be doing in this chapter.

In this section, we will introduce the layer object n the ArcGIS Javascript API, an important object that we will be using to query for features to answer interesting questions.

The Feature Layer Object

The mapview object contains one active map. The map object contains one or more layers. Most of our work in this book will be against the layer object to perform different queries and filtering. The feature layer object is our gate to this resource. Let us see how we can get the layers off the map object.

Open Visual Studio Code on your project folder, you can sync up with our last state of the code here https://github.com/hnasr/gisprogrammingbook/tree/ch3-5. Remember you can always start from any chapter if you want to, copy the code from the URL above, create a new folder and past all the files. Run **npm test** and you are good to go. Contact me if you are running into any sort of problems. Twitter @hnasr or email hus.mhd@gmail.com

In the map object, there is an array called "layers" we will get that array and just ask for its length property which will tell us how many layers are in the map. Let's write these line of code …

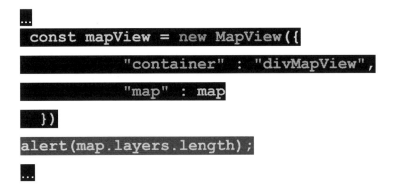

```
...
const mapView = new MapView({
            "container" : "divMapView",
            "map" : map
    })
alert(map.layers.length);
...
```

Save and run your code by accessing http://localhost:8080

At first, you might think this is little odd to get zero, we do have one layer called Landmarks. But if you really think about it, the alert code is executing BEFORE the map actually finished loading, this is back to our Promise discussion in chapter 2. We need to tell the map object, hey, whenever you are done, tell me how many layers do I have. How do we do that? Using promises.

```
const mapView = new MapView({
        "container" : "divMapView",
        "map" : map
})
map.when(() => alert(map.layers.length))
```

Save and run your code, now we clearly see that the number if correct. If you even pay more attention to the page you can see the map is loaded in the background while it was not in the previous screenshot.

Note: In Javascript 4.9 the Map and MapView object are using "when" method to return the promise instead of then.

Let us find out what is the layer name now. We will need to get the first layer using the [0], then use the title property on the map.

```
map.when(() => alert(map.layers.items[0].title))
```

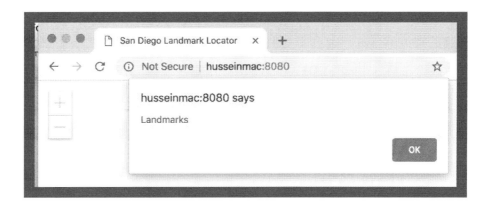

Let us remove this code since we don't want that ugly box to show up every time we load the page. You can simply comment the code which tells the browser to ignore it by adding // it will turn green indicating this is a comment. Or you can simply remove it, your call.

```
//map.when(() => alert(map.layers.items[0].title))
```

Note: There are other cool properties to the layer that we will explore in the coming series. Here is the complete list of the layer properties from Esri site.
https://developers.arcgis.com/javascript/latest/api-reference/esri-layers-FeatureLayer.html

Building the Toolbar

Before we start working with our map and layers we need to build the tooltip bar, which will be a strip on the top of the page where all our tools will go including our first one, the layers list. Let us add the toolbar div element in your <body> tag.

```
...
<body>
    <div id = 'divMapView'></div>
    <div id = 'divToolbar'>this is my toolbar</div>
</body>
...
```

The toolbar really does nothing without a style, let us add some CSS style to it. Let go to the <style> section of your HTML file and add a **#divToolbar.** This tells the page to apply this style to the element with the id "divToolbar". We will add 5 important properties, the first one is **position:fixed** which tells it to always stays in its place regardless whether we scroll the page or not. Top:0 which sets it on top of the page and width:100% which sets it to fill the entire width of the page. The background becomes black and the font is white.

```
<style>
html,
body,
#divMapView {
    padding: 0;
    margin: 0;
    width:100%;
    height:100%;
}
#divToolbar {
    top:0;
    width:100%;
    position: fixed;
    background:black;
    color: white;
}
</style>
```

Save and refresh your page.

The toolbar is not bad, I just prefer it is was transparent so I can actually see the portion of the map it covers. Small change to the background to use **rgba** method with 0, 0, 0 and 60% transparency.

```
#divToolbar {
        top:0;
        width:100%;
        position: fixed;
        background:rgba(0,0,0,0.6);
        color: white;
}
```

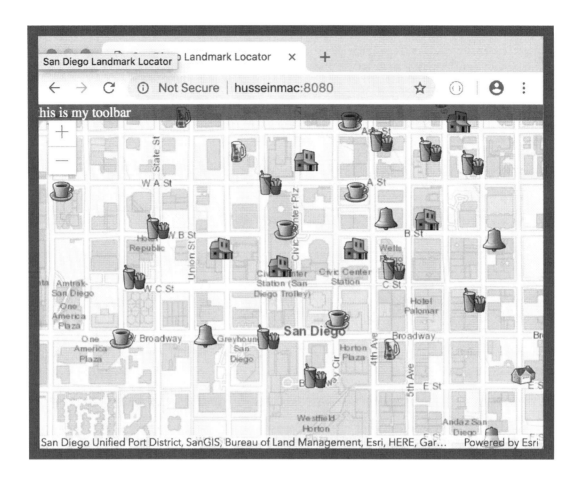

Populate the Layers in a drop-down list

In this section, we will read all the layers available in the map and populate it in a drop-down list using its title. This is a good general practice in case you have multiple layers in the map. This drop-down list will be our context for what layer is active. In this example, we don't really need to do that but it is a best practice give a user a way to see all the layers in the map.

We will create the select HTML element which will be our drop-down list for the layers. In your toolbar div element add the select element. Let us call the new element **ddLayerList**. P.s. remove the *This is my toolbar text.* We will also add a Layers label before the drop-down list.

```
<div id = 'divMapView'></div>
    <div id = 'divToolbar'>
```

```
        <label>Layers</label>
            <select id = 'ddLayerList'>
            </select>
        </div>
```

Save and refresh the page.

You can now see the Layers drop-down list, however, it is empty. We will need to populate it with our layers.

Let us attempt to populate the layers in the drop-down list. First little javascript exercise, how about we populate the list with a fake array first? Go to the beginning of your <script> tag and let us define a new function called **loadLayers**. This will be the function that we call to populate our layers from the map.

```
<script>
    function loadLayers() {
```

```
        }
    require (["esri/WebMap", "esri/views/MapView"],
...
```

For now, we will simply create one item in the drop-down list, to do that we need to get a reference to the ddLayerList element, create an "option" element, set its text to anything, append it to the dropdown list.

```
function loadLayers() {
    let ddLayerList = document.getElementById("ddLayerList");
    let o = document.createElement("option");
    o.textContent = "Layer 1";
    ddLayerList.appendChild(o)
}
```

Our function is ready to be tested, but we need to call it, do you remember how to call a function when the map is ready? Yes, promises! Add this code to your **require** function.

```
const mapView = new MapView({
    "container" : "divMapView",
    "map" : map
    })
    map.when(() => loadLayers())
})
</script>
```

Refresh the page. You can see "Layer 1" showing in the drop-down list.

Let us change this so it actually loops through the map object layers list and populate the layers. We will need to add a parameter to the function called layers and use the forEach loop to loop through all layers as we learned in chapter 2.

```
function loadLayers(layers) {
    layers.forEach(l => {
        let ddLayerList = document.getElementById("ddLayerList");
        let o = document.createElement("option");
        o.textContent = l.title;
        ddLayerList.appendChild(o)
    });
}
```

Finally, we pass the loadLayers function the layers list from the map.

```
map.when(() => loadLayers(map.layers))
```

That is more like it. It now says Landmarks.

For performance reasons, it is better to take out **getElementById** method from the loop since we only need to call it once and since we know it is not going to change we can use const instead of let.

```
function loadLayers(layers) {
    const ddLayerList = document.getElementById("ddLayerList");
    layers.forEach(l => {
        let o = document.createElement("option");
        o.textContent = l.title;
        ddLayerList.appendChild(o)
    });
}
```

I also want to add another function to retrieve the active layer. In order to do that, each drop-down list item should reference its layer. To do that we need to add one more line to our loadLayers function. This is another cool thing about javascript, we can add dynamic properties to any object.

```
    function loadLayers(layers) {
        const ddLayerList = document.getElementById("ddLayerList");
        layers.forEach(l => {
            let o = document.createElement("option");
            o.textContent = l.title;
            o.layer = l;
            ddLayerList.appendChild(o)
        });
    }
```

Finally, we will write a function that returns the active layer, get a reference of the layer drop-down list, get the currently selected index and return the layer.

```
function getActiveLayer () {
    const ddLayerList =
document.getElementById("ddLayerList");
    const selectedIndex = ddLayerList.options.selectedIndex;
    return ddLayerList.options[selectedIndex].layer;
}
```

Here is the source code so far https://github.com/hnasr/gisprogrammingbook/tree/ch4-1

Query Feature Count

In this section, we will build a drop-down list of all the available types in our landmarks layer and when the user selects a type we will show how many features of that type available in the layer.

Building the Types drop-down list

In this section, we will build the landmark types list. Later we will populate this dynamically with the unique list of types that we have.

Go to your <body> tag and add a label and a dropdown list for the types and another label for the type count which we will use to populate the type count in.

```
<div id = 'divToolbar'>
        <label>Layers</label>
        <select id = 'ddLayerList'>
        </select>
        <label>Types</label>
        <select id = 'ddTypeList'>
        </select>
        <label id = 'lblTypeCount'></label>
    </div>
```

Just like we wrote a function to load the layers, we need another function to load the types. For now, we will hard code those types, later we will dynamically query the layer and find all its types. Go to the **<script>** tag and add the loadTypes function, the code is very similar to the load layer function.

```
function loadLandmarkTypes() {
        const ddTypeList = document.getElementById("ddTypeList");
        const types = ['library', 'restaurant', 'cafe', 'school',
'bar', 'hospital']
        types.forEach(t => {
            let o = document.createElement("option");
            o.textContent = t;
            ddTypeList.appendChild(o)
        })
    }
```

We need to call the function just like we did with load layers.

```
map.when(() => {
            loadLayers(map.layers);
            loadLandmarkTypes();
        })
```

Save your work and refresh the page you can now see the list of landmark types.

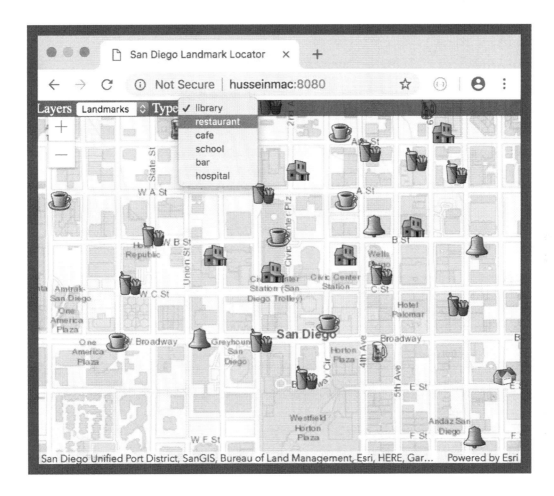

Querying the number of features in a given Type

Now that we have the type ready, we want to actually do something when the user selects a type. Two things here, we will add a "change" event to our drop-down list, which is just telling the browser, if someone changes the drop-down list item run some code. Second thing, when the user changes the type, we will query the number of features in the landmarks layer having that type. Let us add the event first, in the promise when the map is ready, get the types drop-down list then call addEventListener on the change command, pass in the function that you would like the browser to call when the user changes type.

```
map.when(() => {
        loadLayers(map.layers);
        loadLandmarkTypes();
        //setup events
        const ddTypeList =
document.getElementById("ddTypeList");
        ddTypeList.addEventListener("change", onTypeChange);
    })
```

Obviously, the onTypeChange function doesn't exist so let us write it. This is a special function called event function, which takes an event object. The event object carries valuable information about the target object, in this case, it is the drop down list itself! So what we want to do as a start is just alert and show the currently selected type when the user changes the type.

```
function onTypeChange(e) {
    const dd = e.target;
    const selectedIndex = dd.options.selectedIndex;
    alert(dd.options[selectedIndex].textContent);
}
```

Save your work and refresh the page, select a type and see the alert box shows up. In this screenshot the type was set the hospital, I changed it to **bar** so I get the alert box first then the dropdown changes.

Now that we know our event is working, time to query the layer. We need to introduce a new object called the query object which will give us the ability to define query parameters, the one we are interested in here is where which is the filter.

We will need to first get the active layer first, remember the function we authored in the beginning of this chapter, which will return the feature layer, then we will call createQuery which will create a query object. I saved the type object into a constant to avoid writing this long string dd.options...

```
function onTypeChange(e) {
    const dd = e.target;
    const selectedIndex = dd.options.selectedIndex;
    const type = dd.options[selectedIndex].textContent;
    const landmarkLayer = getActiveLayer();
    const query = landmarkLayer.createQuery();
    query.where = "Type = '" + type + "'";
}
```

The final step is to call the queryFeatureCount function, pass it the query. This function returns a promise which will then call our function which in this case just alerts the number.

```
function onTypeChange(e) {
    const dd = e.target;
    const selectedIndex = dd.options.selectedIndex;
    const type = dd.options[selectedIndex].textContent;
    const landmarkLayer = getActiveLayer();
    const query = landmarkLayer.createQuery();
    query.where = "Type = '" + type + "'";
    landmarkLayer.queryFeatureCount(query).then(c =>
alert(c));
}
```

Save your work and refresh the page. Change the type and see how now you are getting the count of each landmark type. As illustrated in this screenshot we have 6 cafes

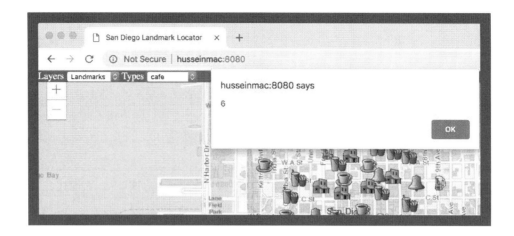

Note: Learn more about the query object here
https://developers.arcgis.com/javascript/latest/api-reference/esri-tasks-support-Query.html

Alerts are useful for quick testing, but they are annoying so we need to show that number on the toolbar. Remember we had an element called lblTypeCount, let's use it to show the count instead.

```
function onTypeChange(e) {
    . . . . . . . . . . . .
    query.where = "Type = '" + type + "'";
    landmarkLayer.queryFeatureCount(query).then(c => {
        const lblTypeCount = document.getElementById("lblTypeCount");
        lblTypeCount.textContent = c;
    });
}
```

It is recommended when using promise to catch for failures, this function getFeatureCount is not always guaranteed to success, sometimes you lose interest connectivity, something happens at the server, or the map becomes unavailable. So let us add a catch phrase to our promise in case of failure and just show an alert message just in case.

```
landmarkLayer.queryFeatureCount(query)
        .then(c => {
            const lblTypeCount =
document.getElementById("lblTypeCount");
            lblTypeCount.textContent = c;
        })
        .catch(e => alert("Error executing function."))
        . . . . . . . . . . .
```

You can find the latest code here https://github.com/hnasr/gisprogrammingbook/tree/ch4-2

Filtering Map based on a Query

We learned how to get the number of features using a query object. In this section, we will filter the map to only show the selected type. For instance, if the user select bar, we will only show the bars in the map and so on. For this, we will introduce the definition expression.

Filter the Map on Type change

One of the properties in the feature layer is called **definitionExpression**, setting this to a where clause will help us filter the layer so it only shows features that satisfy that condition.

We almost have all the pieces in place adding this will be simple. You might have guessed where we need to add this code. Since we need to filter the map when the type change, we will need to add it to onTypeChange function. Since the expression is exactly the same as the **query.where** string we will simply use that.

```
function onTypeChange(e) {
    . . . . . . . . . . .
    const query = landmarkLayer.createQuery();
    query.where = "Type = '" + type + "'";
    landmarkLayer.definitionExpression = query.where;
    landmarkLayer.queryFeatureCount(query)
    . . . . . . . . . . .
}
```

Save your work and refresh the page. This is exciting!

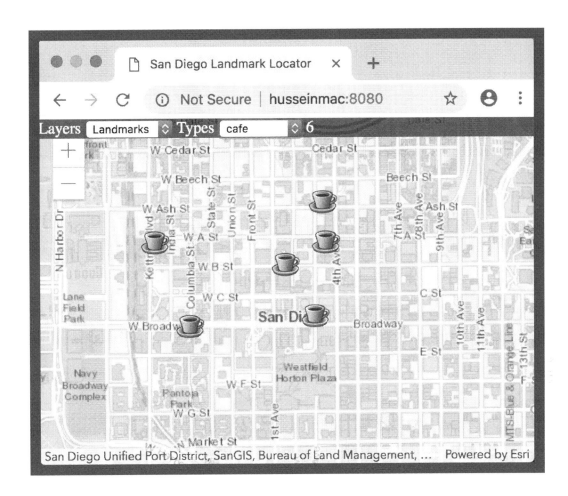

Adding the All option

You may have already noticed once you select a type and filter the map on it, you can't go back to the default view which lists all types or clear that filter. What we are missing in the Types drop-down list is All option. Let's add that, go to your loadLandmarkTypes function and add a new option called All to your list.

```
function loadLandmarkTypes() {
    const ddTypeList = document.getElementById("ddTypeList");
    const types = ['All', 'library', 'restaurant', 'cafe',
'school', 'bar', 'hospital']
    types.forEach(t => {
        let o = document.createElement("option");
        o.textContent = t;
        ddTypeList.appendChild(o)
```

```
        })

    }
```

We know need to add some logic to our onTypeChange function so that if the user selects "All" we want the query to return essentially everything in it. To do that we need to pass an expression that is always true, **1 = 1**, **7 > 0**, **1 < 9** anything that is always true will work. I'm going to use 1=1

```
function onTypeChange(e) {
    . . . . . . . . . . .
        const query = landmarkLayer.createQuery();
        if (type == "All")
            query.where = "1=1";
        else
            query.where = "Type = '" + type + "'";
        landmarkLayer.definitionExpression = query.where;
    . . . . . . . . . . .
```

Save your work and run.

Query Distinct

So far we hard-coded the types in the drop-down list. This is fine and will work until someone decided to introduce a new type in the data if someone did that we need to modify the code and that is inconvenient. We want to make the code smart enough to always read the types from the layer. In this section, we will populate the landmarks types dynamically by doing a distinct query.

Query.returnDistinctValues

To perform a distinct query, we need to set certain parameters first. The first question is what is the field that we want distinctly returned? Simple, it is the type field, we need to set the outFields array property, second since we don't really care about the geometry we will ask the query object not to bother returning the geometry, this is to achieve better performance since geometries are expensive to build. Finally, we set the option to return distinct values. This query will get executed on the server and we will only get the unique values of the type field. Go to the Here is the code to query that query object.

```
function loadLandmarkTypes() {
    const ddTypeList = document.getElementById("ddTypeList");
    const landmarkLayer = getActiveLayer();
    const query = landmarkLayer.createQuery();
    query.outFields = ["type"];
    query.returnGeometry = false;
    query.returnDistinctValues = true;
    const types = ['All', 'library', 'restaurant', 'cafe',
'school', 'bar', 'hospital']
    ....
```

Next, we will execute the **queryFeature** function on the layer passing our new query object, this will return a promise with the list of features. Each **Feature** (or **Graphic** as called in API) has certain properties such as geometries and attributes, but we are interested in the attributes object which will be the access to our Type field. We can safely remove the Type array and reuse the forEach loop.

```
function loadLandmarkTypes() {
    . . . . . . . . . . .
    query.returnGeometry = false;
    query.returnDistinctValues = true;
    landmarkLayer.queryFeatures(query)
        .then(result => result.features.forEach(t => {
            let o = document.createElement("option");
            o.textContent = t.attributes.Type;
            ddTypeList.appendChild(o)
        }))
        .catch(e => alert("Error executing query."));

}
```

Learn more about the properties of a feature (graphic) here
https://developers.arcgis.com/javascript/latest/api-reference/esri-Graphic.html

Save your work and refresh! Now you can see the list is populated. However we are missing something, the All is gone, we need to add it back. One easy way to do this is to add it at the beginning of the loadLandmarkTypes function.

```
function loadLandmarkTypes() {
    . . . . . . . . . . . .
    query.returnGeometry = false;
    query.returnDistinctValues = true;
    const oAll = document.createElement("option");
    oAll.textContent = "All";
    ddTypeList.appendChild(oAll);
    landmarkLayer.queryFeatures(query)
    .then(result => result.features.forEach(t => {
    . . . . . . . . . . . .
    }
```

Although your application doesn't look much different, you did make great improvements to your code.

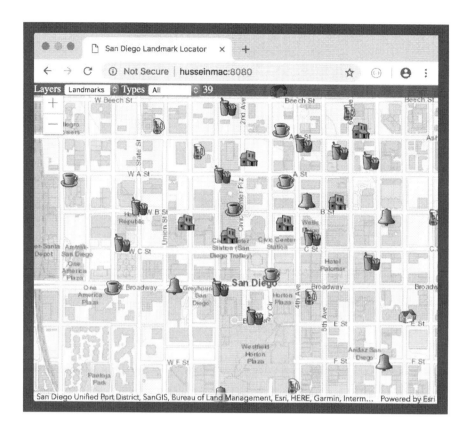

You can find the latest code for this section here
https://github.com/hnasr/gisprogrammingbook/tree/ch4-3

Query Features

In this section, we will develop a search by landmark name functionality. We will build a new text box control and when we type in a search term and hit enter we will query and populate a limited list with the search results. When the user clicks on a result we will zoom to the feature.

Building a search text box and results

First, we need to build some style for our search box and results. Most popular sites put their search box on the top right so let us do that. Head to your <style> tag and add the following classes. First, the search box which will be applied to the search box. I want the width to be 100, set it to the most right by setting right to zero, the position is absolute so it is positioned related to the parent, which is the toolbar div. And finally some colors. Second for the searchResult class which will be applied to the search result div element. Same thing almost just with a height that holds at least 3 results. We don't want to list everything.

...

```css
.searchBox {
        width:100px;
        right:0;
        position: absolute;
        background-color: rgba(255,255,255);
        color: black;
    }
    .searchResult {
        width:100px;
        height:60px;
        right:0;
        position: absolute;
        background-color: rgba(255,255,255);
        color: black;
    }


    </style>
```

Note: Notice that a class starts with a "." while styling a specific element starts with a #.

Now head to your <body> section and add two new elements, a text box, and a new div, both having the class search.

```html
    <div id = 'divToolbar'>
        . . . . . . . . . .
        <label id = 'lblTypeCount'></label>
        <input type = 'text' id = 'txtSearch' class =
'searchBox'>
        <div id = 'divSearchResults' class = 'searchResult'>
            search result 1
            search result 2
            search result 3
```

```
        </div>
    </div>
```

Save your work and run take a look at your page. You should see the new text box and the search result.

What we want to do is to hide that search result box until the user actually types something. Let us hide that search result div element. Simply add the **display:none** to the searchResult class.

```
.searchResult {
    display:none;
    width:100px;
    height:60px;
    right:0;
    position: absolute;
    background-color: rgba(255,255,255);
    color: black;
}
```

Now you should see that the results are hidden. To show those result we need to add an event so that when we type something in search box we show the box. Let us wire the event, the event name is called keypress, which means any key pressed while the textbox is active will activate that event and call the function you specified. Go to the require function, look for map.when and add the code for the event. We will call a new function called **onSearch**.

```javascript
map.when(() => {
    //map is ready
    loadLayers(map.layers);
    loadLandmarkTypes();
    //setup events
    const ddTypeList = document.getElementById("ddTypeList");
    const txtSearch = document.getElementById("txtSearch");
    ddTypeList.addEventListener("change", onTypeChange);
    txtSearch.addEventListener("keypress", onSearch);
})
```

As usual, **onSearch** function doesn't exist so we need to write it, go to the top of your <script> tag and add it.

```javascript
<script>
    function onSearch (e) {
    }
    function onTypeChange(e) {
        . . . . . . . . . .
```

For now, we simply want to show the search Results if it is not already visible.

```javascript
    function onSearch (e) {
        const divSearchResults =
document.getElementById("divSearchResults");
        divSearchResults.style.display = "block";
    }
```

Great! When we load the page and lwe don't see the result, as we start to type something the result box shows up.

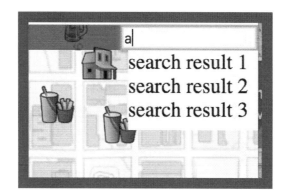

However, there is an optimization we can do here. So far we didn't have to do that for other elements and every time we need an element we call document.getElementById. However, the divSearchResults element is a busy element. Remember we are calling it everytime we type anything, we are calling it everytime we leave the box. So it is recommended to save a modular reference to this element and use it across all our script. In the begging of your script declare a new object for the divSearchResult.

```
<script>
    let divSearchResults;
    function onSearch (e) {
        ......
```

Add an initializing code and let's replace all the occurrences with this object. We have one on the onSearch method and another one focus out.

```
//setup events
const ddTypeList = document.getElementById("ddTypeList");
const txtSearch = document.getElementById("txtSearch");
divSearchResults = document.getElementById("divSearchResults");
```

This is the last code so far for this section.
https://github.com/hnasr/gisprogrammingbook/tree/ch4-4

Query with LIKE clause

We have made the necessary setup code for our search box and results. It is time to execute the query. Since we are planning to search the landmarks by name in this method, we want to return any landmark that contains the user search term. For that, we use the **LIKE** keyword in our where clause with the % wildcard. For example, Adding **bar%** will return all landmarks that start with **bar** and end with anything else, so bar station, bar nation. Adding %bar will return all landmarks that end with bar and start with anything, ocean bar, sea bar, etc. Adding %bar% will return all landmarks that have the word bar in it regardless of where. That is what we will use.

In the **onSearch** function, we will build a query object, send it to the queryFeatures function and populate the divSearchResults with new list item that we create on the fly. The "**li**" element is an HTML list item which helps us create a bulleted list.

```javascript
function onSearch (e) {
    divSearchResults.style.display = "block";
    const q = e.target.value;
    const landmarkLayer = getActiveLayer();
    const query = landmarkLayer.createQuery();
    query.where = "Name like '%" + q + "%'";
    query.returnGeometry=false;
    landmarkLayer.queryFeatures(query)
    .then(result => result.features.forEach(f => {
        let r = document.createElement("li")
        r.textContent = f.attributes.Name;
        divSearchResults.appendChild(r);
    }))
    .catch(e => alert ("Error executing query " + e));
}
```

Save your work and run. We immediately see results, but they don't look as good as we anticipated. Can you think why?

First, we are not clearly the search results elements, we keep adding to it. Second, we return a lot of results, we need a way to tell the query to only return 3 results. Finally, we want to execute this code only to enter not as we type. Fortunately, both things are simple, we can clear the results by clearing the innerHTML and we can limit the query by setting the num parameter. Here is the updated code.

```
function onSearch (e) {
    ............................ .
    query.num = 3;
    divSearchResults.innerHTML = "";
    landmarkLayer.queryFeatures(query)
    ............................ .
}
```

Finally, we want to only execute the query when the user actually hits enter, this way we don't bombard the server with lots of queries which will slow down our app. We can use event argument to get the code which is which key is currently being pressed. If it is anything other than **enter**, just exit the function.

```
function onSearch (e) {
    if (e.code != "Enter") return;
```

Save your code and open your application. Type in **cave** and hit enter, you should now see 3 results only. Experiment with your new search capability.

You can find the latest code with these changes here
https://github.com/hnasr/gisprogrammingbook/tree/ch4-5

Zoom to feature

Now that we are listing the search results, we want to add our final touch to zoom to the feature when the user clicks on the result. To achieve that we want to we need to add a click event on the list item, use the **mapview** object to goTo the feature geometry. Let us add a click event to the list element to call a function **zoomTo** when the user clicks on the list item. We also want to save the feature in the list element object so we can use it later. Go to the **onSearch** function and add the following two lines.

```
.then(result => result.features.forEach(f => {
    let r = document.createElement("li")
    r.textContent = f.attributes.Name;
    r.feature = f;
```

```
            r.addEventListener("click", zoomTo);
            divSearchResults.appendChild(r);
        }))
    .catch(e => alert ("Error executing query " + e));
```

Since **zoomTo** is a new function, let us add it, go to the beginning of the script.

```
    <script>
    let divSearchResults;
    function zoomTo(e) {
    }
```

To zoom to a feature we need to take its geometry and send it to the mapView.goTo function. We also have to change the zoom level of the **mapview** so we can see it up close.

```
    function zoomTo(e) {
        const feature = e.target.feature;
        mapView.zoom = 20;
        mapView.goTo(feature.geometry);
    }
```

There is a slight problem with this code, our browser claim that it can't reach **mapView** object. This is a problem because the mapView object is defined under the require function and we are on a completely different function. So we can define the mapView object as a modular object like divSearchResults element, that will solve this but we will explore another option just to show you guys that there are many ways to solve a problem with coding.

Go to your require function where we defined the mapView object and add this line. This will save the mapView object to the window object which is a global object that can be accessed anywhere in our script.

```
    …….
const mapView = new MapView({
        "container" : "divMapView",
        "map" : map
    })
    window.mapView = mapView;
    map.when(() => {
    …….
```

Go back to your **zoomTo** function and add an extra constant referencing your window.mapView.

```
function zoomTo(e) {
        const mapView = window.mapView;
        const feature = e.target.feature;
        mapView.zoom = 20;
        mapView.goTo(feature.geometry);
    }
```

Run your code! Type cave and click on Roans Cave result, and we are in the middle of the ocean! That doesn't look right

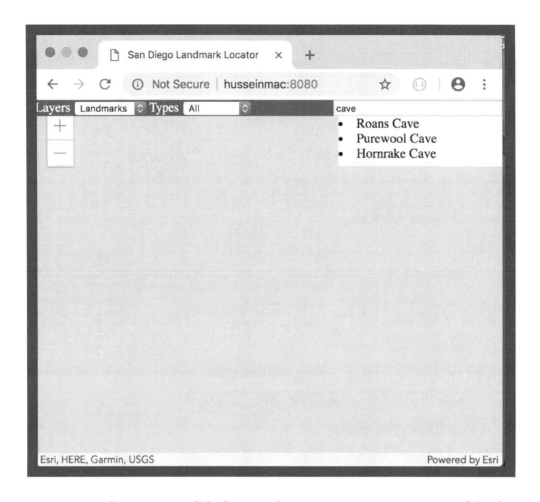

The reason we got an incorrect result is that we chose not to return geometry of the feature when we did the search in the **onSearch** function. Simple fix, go to your onSearch function and set the **returnGeometry** to true.

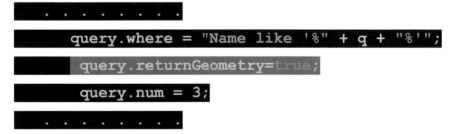

```
        . . . . . . .
        query.where = "Name like '%" + q + "%'";
        query.returnGeometry=true;
        query.num = 3;
        . . . . . . . .
```

Re-run your code, search hit enter and click on Roans Cave, notice now that we are zooming in to the result.

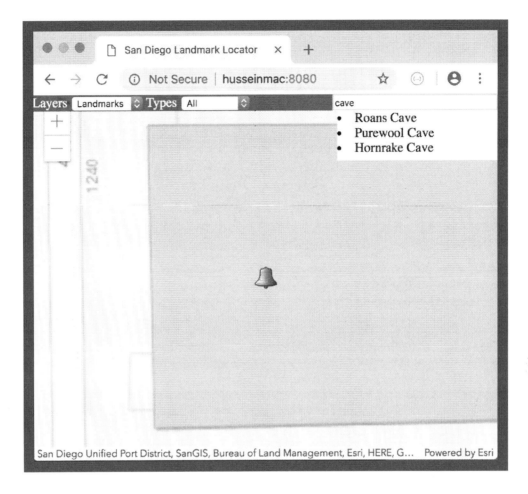

You can find the final code for this chapter here
https://github.com/hnasr/gisprogrammingbook/tree/ch4-6

Summary

In this chapter, we have built basic search capability. We learned about the feature layer and the different query methods. We built a user experience for the user to interact with where we listed all the layers in the map. We then listed all the different types of landmarks in the layer by doing a distinct query. We learned about definition expression in the layer and how can we use it to filter results on the map. Finally, we have built the search by name using a bounded query to return certain number rows from the query, and we implemented a zoom to feature method to take the feature geometry and zoom to it.

Chapter 5: Spatial Search

We are reaching an end of the book, it is was a great journey for me and I hope for you too. I wanted to conclude the book last chapter with the most exciting features. Spatial operations. In this chapter, we will build the spatial component of our landmark locator. We will learn how to create points, lines, and polygons, we will learn how to execute spatial searches and answer interesting questions such as are there are any liquor stores within a 1000 feet of a school, list all cafes next to a particular restaurant and so on. We will also learn to search landmarks within the current extent.

Here is an example of what you will be able to do by the end of the chapter.

- Customizing Popup
  - Popup Templates
  - Building the Popup UX (Type, Distance, Button)
- Spatial Query and Graphics
  - Geometry Service
  - Create Buffer
  - Use Geometry Service To Create Buffer
  - Creating Polygon Graphic
  - Intersect Query
  - Create Point Graphic
  - Additional Filtering
  - Create Line Graphic
  - Calculating Distance and Creating Text Graphic
- Search By Extent

Customizing Popup

You may have noticed when we load our application and click on a landmark we get a dialog which shows basic details about that landmarks as illustrated below. This is called a popup and by default, we get this default attribute popup.

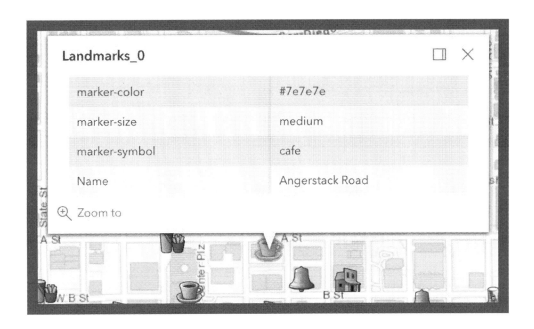

Luckily Popups are customizable via popup templates, we will create our own popup template that has some controls which will allow us to interact with the application. We want to a text box where the user can type distance in feet, we want a drop-down list of all types of landmarks and finally, we want a button that allows us to create a buffer circle around the selected landmark and highlights all nearby landmarks based on the selected type. Don't worry if this sound confusing it will clear itself out as we progress.

Popup Templates

Popup templates can be set at the layer to control the dialog that displays when a user clicks on a feature within that layer. A Popup template is a JSON object with a lot of parameters, we are interested in two, Title which is the title of the popup and Content which represents the content of the popup. The Content can be a string, an array of objects, promise or a function that returns HTML element. In this chapter, we will use a function as content which gives us the most control. The function content takes a feature as a parameter which is the feature the user interacted with and returns an HTML element. Open your code on Index.html and head to the **map.when** function. If you skipped directly to this chapter don't worry, you can always pick up from the latest source code on chapter 4 here
https://github.com/hnasr/gisprogrammingbook/tree/ch4-6

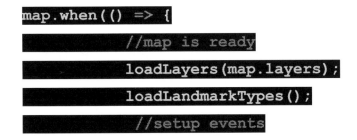

```
map.when(() => {
        //map is ready
        loadLayers(map.layers);
        loadLandmarkTypes();
        //setup events
```

```
        const ddTypeList =
document.getElementById("ddTypeList");
        const txtSearch =
document.getElementById("txtSearch");
        divSearchResults =
document.getElementById("divSearchResults");
        ddTypeList.addEventListener("change", onTypeChange);
        txtSearch.addEventListener("keypress", onSearch);
        //create custom popup

    })
```

We will get the active layer and set the **popupTemplate** property as follows.

```
//create custom popup
        let landmarkLayer = getActiveLayer();
        landmarkLayer.popupTemplate = {
            "title": "My Custom Template",
            "content": feature => {
            }
        }
```

Let us return a div element that has a label and simple dropdown list for illustration purposes.

```
        landmarkLayer.popupTemplate = {
            "title": "My Custom Template",
            "content": feature => {
//return a div element and a drop down list with a text element
                const dv = document.createElement("div");
                const dd = document.createElement("select");
```

```javascript
        const o = document.createElement("option");
        const tx = document.createTextNode("Sample");
        o.textContent = "sample";
        dd.appendChild(o)
        dv.appendChild(tx);
        dv.appendChild(dd);
        return dv;
    }
}
```

Save your work and run npm test then click on a feature, you will notice a completely different popup. My Custom Template on the title

By using curly braces you can access the field values of the landmark being selected. This is how you show the name of the landmark for example

```javascript
//create custom popup
        let landmarkLayer = getActiveLayer();
        landmarkLayer.popupTemplate = {
            "title": "My Custom Template - {Name}",
            "content": feature => {
```

You can find the source code for the code we just wrote here

https://github.com/hnasr/gisprogrammingbook/tree/ch5-1

Read more about Popup template from the official Esri site
https://developers.arcgis.com/javascript/latest/api-reference/esri-PopupTemplate.html

Building the Popup UX

In this section, we will use the popup template to build our user interface of this chapter. Remember what we are trying to do, we want a user to click on a landmark, and from the popup she can set the text field distance in feet, select a type from a dropdown list and click on a button. When the user clicks on the button, we will create a circle buffer based on the specified distance around the landmark, highlight all landmarks from the type the user selected and calculate the distance between each landmark and the target landmark.

Go back to your code, replace the code of your content function and for now let's just create the distance text box set it to 1000 feet by default.

```
landmarkLayer.popupTemplate = {
        "title": "Find nearby - {Name}",
        "content": feature => {
            //return a div element that has everything
```

```
        const dv = document.createElement("div");
        //distance text box where use will type
        const txtDistance = document.createElement("input");
        txtDistance.type = 'text';
        //default 1000 feet
        txtDistance.value = 1000;
        dv.appendChild(txtDistance);
        return dv;
    }
  }
```

Save your work and run npm test, click on a feature you should see the text box.

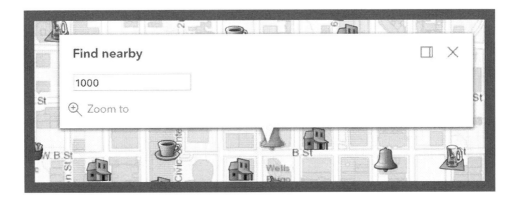

Would be nice to append a text node next to it so we know what this text box is for.

```
//default 1000 feet
txtDistance.value = 1000;
dv.appendChild(document.createTextNode(" Distance: "));
dv.appendChild(txtDistance);
return dv;
```

Much better.

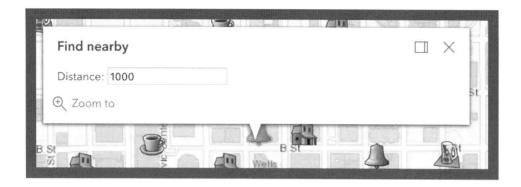

Now let us add the type dropdown list. Remember we already spent some time building that, so all we have to do is just copy it and add it to our popup. This is how you copy an HTML element in javascript. We also want to text node to correctly label it.

```
//default 1000 feet
txtDistance.value = 1000;
//clone the type list
const ddcloneTypes = ddTypeList.cloneNode(true);
dv.appendChild(document.createTextNode(" Type: "))
dv.appendChild(ddcloneTypes);
dv.appendChild(document.createTextNode(" Distance: "));
dv.appendChild(txtDistance);
return dv;
```

Save your work and run it.

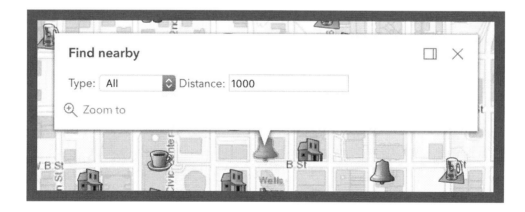

Finally, let us add the search button which we will use later to create the buffer. Also, we want to add a text node to label the distance in feet. The order of appending the controls matter to get a nice view.

```javascript
//clone the type list
const ddcloneTypes = ddTypeList.cloneNode(true);
//create button
const btnSpatialSearch = document.createElement("button");
btnSpatialSearch.textContent = "Search";
dv.appendChild(document.createTextNode(" Type: "))
dv.appendChild(ddcloneTypes);
dv.appendChild(document.createTextNode(" Distance: "));
dv.appendChild(txtDistance);
dv.appendChild(document.createTextNode(" ft. "));
dv.appendChild(btnSpatialSearch);
return dv;
```

Save your run your work.

Obviously, none of the controls do any work but we will plug in the logic in the coming sections.

You can find the source code of this section here
https://github.com/hnasr/gisprogrammingbook/tree/ch5-2

Spatial Query and Graphics

A spatial query is a query that takes as an input a geometry to further filter results based on a spatial operator. For example, you can pass a circle as a geometry to a query on the landmarks table asking to return all landmarks that are within the circle. Graphics are geometries with special symbol allowing them to be rendered on the map. You can create point, line or polygon graphics and assign different symbols to them. In this section, we will explore the spatial query and graphics.

Symbols are used to render geometries into graphics, there are many types of symbols we are mainly interested in three symbols. Fill symbol which is used to render polygon geometries such as circles and rectangles, line symbol for line geometry and marker symbol for points.

Geometry Service

The Geometry Service is a server-side engine that can be used to perform complex spatial operations such as Buffer, Projection, Densify and much more. Spatial operations are expensive that is why we usually perform them on the server and return the results. In this section, we will use the geometry service to perform buffer which will allow us to create a circular fence around the landmark we select. We will then create a graphic and show it on the map.

We will use the GeometryService hosted by Esri here since we are using them for development we should be good.
https://sampleserver6.arcgisonline.com/arcgis/rest/services/Utilities/Geometry/GeometryServer
You can learn more about the Geometry service here
https://developers.arcgis.com/javascript/latest/api-reference/esri-tasks-GeometryService.html

Let us include the necessary classes so can use them later, we will need GeometryService, BufferParameters for creating the buffer and Graphic to create the graphics.

```
require (["esri/WebMap", "esri/views/MapView",
"esri/tasks/GeometryService",
"esri/tasks/support/BufferParameters",
"esri/Graphic"],
    (WebMap,MapView,
    GeometryService,
BufferParameters,
Graphic) => {
```

```
const map = new WebMap({
```

We will be using the **Graphic** class in other functions so let us save it into our window object.

```
const mapView = new MapView({
            "container" : "divMapView",
            "map" : map
        })
window.mapView = mapView;
window.Graphic = Graphic;
        map.when(() => {
```

Create Buffer

To create a buffer using the Geometry Service we will need to pass buffer parameters where we specify the distance, unit and input geometry. Once the operation is complete we will get back a polygon geometry. The buffer parameter supports buffering multiple geometries so you can send it multiple geometries and get back multiple geometries. We will then create a graphic from the polygon geometry. So much stuff coming!

Use Geometry Service To Create Buffer

We want to call the Geometry Service when we click on the Search button. But first, do you remember who to wire the click event? Let's do that.

```
//create button
const btnSpatialSearch = document.createElement("button");
btnSpatialSearch.textContent = "Search";
//wire search event
btnSpatialSearch.addEventListener("click", e => {
            //geometry service code goes here
        })
dv.appendChild(document.createTextNode(" Type: "))
```

First, let us define the geometry service by creating a new geometry service object and pass it the geometry service URL. We will use Esri hosted geometry service.

```
//wire search event.
const geometryServiceUrl =
"https://sampleserver6.arcgisonline.com/arcgis/rest/services/Uti
lities/Geometry/GeometryServer";
btnSpatialSearch.addEventListener("click", e => {
    //geometry service code goes here
    const gs = new GeometryService({url:geometryServiceUrl})
})
```

Then we will construct the buffer parameters, which will be an object which has the distance which will is the text box we created, the geometry which is the geometry of the feature (landmark) we selected, finally the unit which will be feet. Notice that these are arrays indicating that the geometry service supports buffering multiple geometries, we will pass an array with a single value since we only buffering one geometry at a time. We get the feature graphic geometry from feature.graphic.geometry.

```
btnSpatialSearch.addEventListener("click", e => {
    //geometry service code goes here
    const g = feature.graphic.geometry;
    const gs = new GeometryService({url: geometryServiceUrl})
    const bf =    new BufferParameters
({
        distances: [txtDistance.value],
        unit: "feet",
        geometries: [g]
    })
})
```

Now that we have the parameters ready, time to call the geometry service buffer method and pass in the buffer parameter. The buffer method returns a promise so we will need to use **then** to wait for a result. When the promise resolves we will get the polygons and create the polygon graphic, this is a new method that we will create. When the promise fails we will catch it and show an error.

```
btnSpatialSearch.addEventListener("click", e => {
        //geometry service code goes here
      const g = feature.graphic.geometry;
      const gs = new GeometryService({url: geometryServiceUrl})
      const bf =  new BufferParameters
({
            distances: [txtDistance.value],
            unit: "feet",
            geometries: [g]
        })
        gs.buffer(bf)
        .then(polygons => {
            //we got back the buffered polygon
            const buffer = polygons [0];
            createPolygonGraphic(buffer);
        })
        .catch(e => alert("Something wrong happened."))


})
```

Finally, we will create the new method to draw the polygon graphic (circle) on the map. We will implement this next.

```
<script>
    let divSearchResults;
    function createPolygonGraphic(geometry) {
        //create polygon graphic
    }


    function zoomTo(e) {
```

Creating Polygon Graphic

Polygon graphics will be the first type of graphic that we will be creating. So we have the polygon geometry that was built by the geometry service, we will need to create a fill symbol, create the graphic and pass in the geometry. First, we will create a fillSymbol object, the symbol object is a rich object with a lot of knobs that you can set to change the color, size, fill style and much more. Default symbols will be black with little transparency and that works for us. Second we want to create a graphic object, pass it the geometry and the symbol and finally, we take the graphic object and add it to the map view.

```
function createPolygonGraphic(geometry) {
    //create polygon graphic
    const fillSymbol = {
        type: "simple-fill"
    }
    const mapview = window.mapView;
    let graphic = new window.Graphic({geometry: geometry,
symbol: fillSymbol})
    mapview.graphics.add(graphic);
}
```

It is been a while since we run the app and we wrote a lot of code, save your work and run it. Click on a landmark and then click **Search** you should see a black transparent circle around the landmark you clicked.

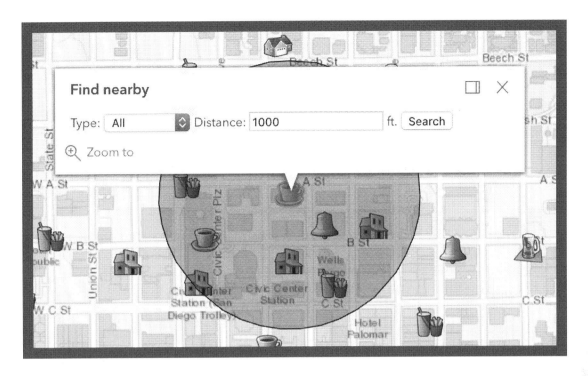

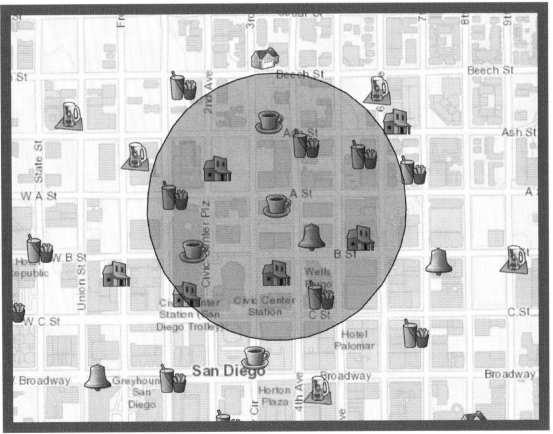

Don't worry if you ran into trouble, you can find the code here and check your work.
https://github.com/hnasr/gisprogrammingbook/tree/ch5-3

Feel free to explore the symbol parameters here, change the color, the fill, and much more..
https://developers.arcgis.com/javascript/latest/api-reference/esri-symbols-SimpleFillSymbol.html

You can also watch the youtube video I did here diving deep into the polygon graphic
https://www.youtube.com/watch?v=XF0zJgOaUJU

Intersect Query

Now that we have the circular buffer, we will need to run a query on the landmarks feature layer and return the results. We know how to create a query, making a spatial query is just a regular query with the input geometry as follows. For simplicity, we will just show the number of features returned.

```javascript
gs.buffer(bf)
    .then(polygons => {
        //we got back the buffered polygon
        const buffer = polygons [0];
        createPolygonGraphic(buffer);
        //query landmarks layer and bass the buffer
        const landmarkLayer = getActiveLayer();
        const q = landmarkLayer.createQuery();
        q.geometry = buffer;
        landmarkLayer.queryFeatures(q)
        .then (result => {
            //do something with the results
            alert(result.features.length)
        })
        .catch (e => alert("error querying features."))
    })
    .catch(e => alert("Something wrong happened."))
```

Save and run your work notice that you started to get a popup with a number of features returned. If you counted the number of landmarks within the circle you will notice that they matched. We just did a spatial query!

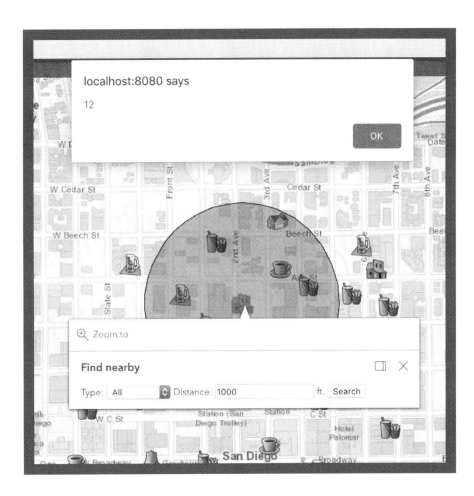

We also want to create graphics for those landmarks that got returned in the result. We will loop through the results and create point graphic for each one of them.

```
landmarkLayer.queryFeatures(q)
    .then (result => {
        //do something with the results
        result.features.forEach(f => {
            //create point graphic
            createPointGraphic(f.geometry)
        });
    })
    .catch (e => alert("error querying features."))
```

Let us stub out the CreatePointGraphic function to be ready to write it.

```
<script>
    let divSearchResults;
    function createPointGraphic(geometry) {
        //create point graphic
    }
    function createPolygonGraphic(geometry) {
```

Create Point Graphic

Now that we have the result of all landmarks within the buffer we need to create a point graphic for each one of them. For polygon graphics we needed a fill symbol, for the point graphic we need a marker symbol.

```
function createPointGraphic(geometry) {
    //create point graphic
    const markerSymbol = {
        type: "simple-marker"
    }
    const mapview = window.mapView;
    let graphic = new window.Graphic({geometry: geometry,
symbol: markerSymbol})
    mapview.graphics.add(graphic);
}
```

Save and run your work.

Default symbols aren't going to cut it for this, I think we need to change it. Let's make it red with some transparency and slightly bigger size?

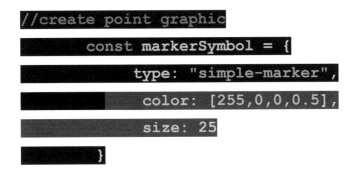

```
//create point graphic
    const markerSymbol = {
        type: "simple-marker",
        color: [255,0,0,0.5],
        size: 25
    }
```

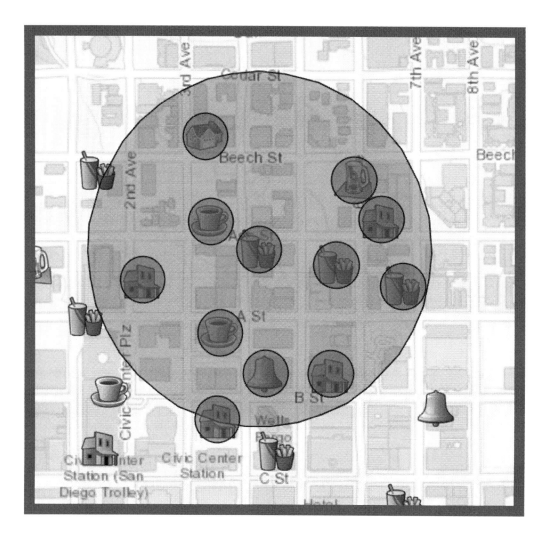

Much better! Feel free to change that to suit your needs.

Here is the source code so far.
https://github.com/hnasr/gisprogrammingbook/tree/ch5-4

Additional Filtering

If you noticed, we are currently returning all landmark types as a result, we want to honor the type drop-down list. We have done this work before if you remember we just need to add the where clause to filter the type based on whatever the user selects.

```
//query landmarks layer and bass the buffer
const landmarkLayer = getActiveLayer();
const q = landmarkLayer.createQuery();
q.geometry = buffer;
```

```
let type =
ddcloneTypes.options[ddcloneTypes.selectedIndex].textContent;
if (type == "All")
    q.where = "1=1";
else
    q.where = "Type = '" + type + "'";
landmarkLayer.queryFeatures(q)
.
```

Save and run your work, click on a school and then find all bars within 1000 feet.

Amazing how far we got right? Try different combos and answer interesting questions!

Create Line Graphic

The last thing we need to do to finish the spatial query and graphics section is to calculate the distance between the current landmark and all the resulting landmarks of the result. A line needs at least two points to be created. For each returned landmark in the result, we will create a line between the result and the currently selected landmark. Let us stub out our last function for this section the **CreateLineGraphic**. The function takes g which is the current selected landmark geometry and f.geometry which is feature returned as a result, since we are in a loop this is going to create a line for each returned landmark.

```
landmarkLayer.queryFeatures(q)
    .then (result => {
        //do something with the results
        result.features.forEach(f => {
            //create point graphic
            createPointGraphic(f.geometry)
            createLineGraphic(g, f.geometry)
        });
    })
```

Then create the function which takes two point geometries.

```
<script>
    let divSearchResults;
    function createLineGraphic(point1, point2) {
        //create line graphic
    }
    function createPointGraphic(geometry) {
```

The symbol for the line is line symbol however If you think about it, we don't really have the line geometry here we actually need to synthesize the geometry of the line. The Paths property is an array of points which has the x and y for each point. We also need to set the spatialReference property so we can add it to the map view. The rest of the stuff is straightforward.

```
function createLineGraphic(point1, point2) {
```

```javascript
//create line graphic
let lineGeometry = {
    type: "polyline",
    paths: [
        [point1.x, point1.y],
        [point2.x, point2.y]
    ],
    spatialReference: point1.spatialReference
}
const lineSymbol = {
    type: "simple-line"
}
const mapview = window.mapView;
let graphic = new window.Graphic({geometry: lineGeometry, symbol: lineSymbol})
mapview.graphics.add(graphic);
}
```

Save your work and run you now notice lines are created too. Here is a screenshot of all cafes next to a school.

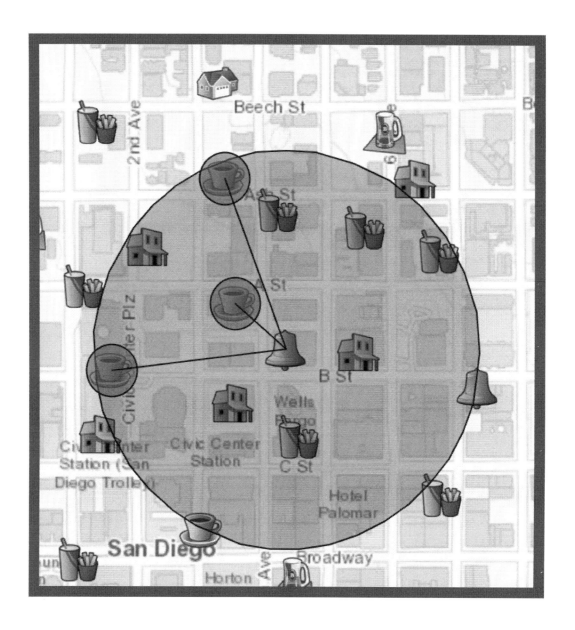

Calculating Distance and Creating Text Graphic

Finally, we want to calculate the line distance and show it on the map. To do that we need to recall some distance formula from high school and we also learn how to create a text graphic to show the distance on the map.

Distance formula between two points P and Q is:

$$d(P,Q) = \sqrt{(x_2 - x_1)^2 + (y_2 - y_1)^2}$$

There is the equivalent javascript for this

```
const distance = Math.sqrt( Math.pow(point2.x - point1.x, 2) +
Math.pow(point2.y - point1.y,2));
```

Now that we have calculated the distance, we will create a text graphic and add it to the resulting landmark. Text graphics are just like any other graphic, they require a symbol and a geometry, the symbol will be text and the geometry will be where that text should show up. Since we want to add the text to the resulting geometry it will be point2. Also since the **spatialReference** of the map is on meters we will need to convert the meters to feet with a simple formula.

```
const mapview = window.mapView;
let graphic = new window.Graphic({geometry: lineGeometry,
symbol: lineSymbol})
mapview.graphics.add(graphic);
//calculate the distance
const distanceMeters = Math.round(Math.sqrt( Math.pow(point2.x -
point1.x, 2) + Math.pow(point2.y - point1.y,2)))
const distanceFeet =  Math.round(3.281 * distanceMeters);
     const textSymbol = {
        type: "text",
        text: distanceFeet + " ft.",
        color: [255,255,255]
     }
let textGraphic = new Graphic({geometry: point2, symbol:
textSymbol});
mapview.graphics.add(textGraphic);
```

Save your work and run it. We can now see the distance on each result.

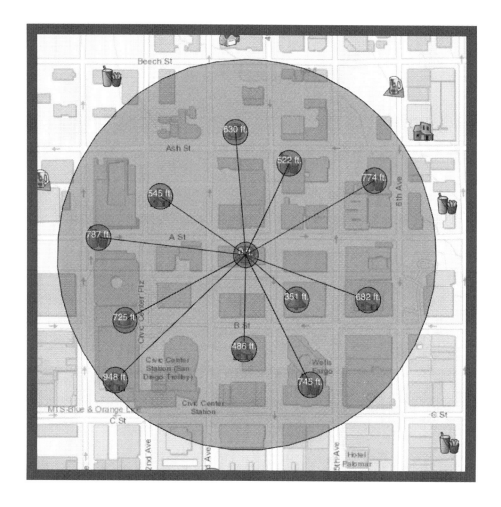

There was a bug that I left until the end to fix if you notice after each search we keep adding new graphics and the old graphics stay. It will be nice to clear the graphics before each search he is how you do it.

Here is the final code for this section https://github.com/hnasr/gisprogrammingbook/tree/ch5-5

Search by Extent

The final piece before we conclude the book is to do a search by extent. Currently, our search by name functionality works on the entire landmark layer. We want to change it so it only displays result within the current display extent. This is similar to how google maps works when you search for something it first tries to show you relevant results near you. Fortunately, this is a one-line fix in the **onSearch** function.

```javascript
function onSearch (e) {
    if (e.code != "Enter") return;
    divSearchResults.style.display = "block";
    const q = e.target.value;
    const landmarkLayer = getActiveLayer();
    const query = landmarkLayer.createQuery();
    query.where = "Name like '%" + q + "%'";
    query.returnGeometry=true;
    query.num = 3;
    query.geometry = window.mapView.extent;
    divSearchResults.innerHTML = "";
    landmarkLayer.queryFeatures(query)
```

Save your work and search for Cave in the full extent, you will get three results.

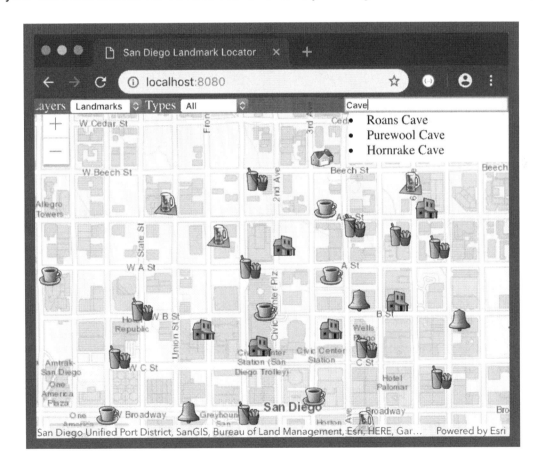

Click on **Roans Cave** which will zoom to the landmark. Then search again for Cave, you will only get that result proving that we are now searching in the current extent.

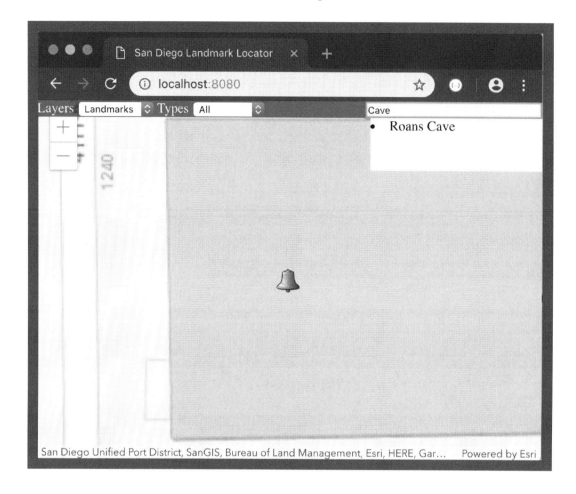

Find the latest code here.

https://github.com/hnasr/gisprogrammingbook/tree/ch5-6

Summary

This was one of the most exciting and longest chapters, we have a learned a lot and you have made it to the end of the book. We have learned about popup templates, customized our landmark layer with its own user experience. We built a user interface for spatial search. We learned all about graphics and created 4 types of graphics, point, line, polygon, and text graphics. We learned about the geometry service and used it to build a buffer around the landmark which then we used to find all landmarks within it. Finally, we performed a search by name within an extent.

This was a very exciting book to write. It has been thrilling to sit down and build out this book. This is my first book to self-publish and not relying on a publisher. If you have purchased this book, I genuinely wish you benefited from this book, thank you very much. Feel free to drop me a line. You have my email. Hus.mhd@gmail.com

Yours
Hussein

Made in the USA
Lexington, KY
19 July 2019